Also by Dave Pelzer

A Child Called "It"

The Lost Boy

A Man Named Dave

Dave Pelzer

DAVE PELZER

HELP YOURSELF

TED SMART

This edition produced for The Book People Ltd,
Hall Wood Avenue, Haydock, St Helens WA11 9UL

Thorsons
An Imprint of HarperCollins*Publishers*
77–85 Fulham Palace Road,
Hammersmith, London W6 8JB

The Thorsons website address is:
www.thorsons.com

First published by Dutton,
a member of Penguin Putnam Inc. 2000
This edition published by Thorsons 2001

1 3 5 7 9 10 8 6 4 2

A catalogue record of this book
is available from the British Library

ISBN 0 00 763947 3

Printed and bound in Great Britain by
Omnia Books Ltd, Glasgow

This book is dedicated to my lovely wife, Marsha, and my incredible son, Stephen, who both guide and inspire me in ways that only God knows.

This book is also dedicated to you, the reader, in the sincere hope that you, too, can live a more fulfilling, productive life that you truly deserve.

Acknowledgments

I wish to take a moment and give thanks to those who contributed to this endeavor. First and foremost my wife—and editor for the fourth time—Marsha, for her fine eye for the written word.

To my research assistant, Rey Thayne, for his endless hours of reverifying "the reverifications" and hunting down the smallest of details to help ensure the validity of the stories.

A special thank you to my personal assistant, Ray Worthington, for keeping chaos in order so as to allow me to scribe at any hour of the day, night, weekends, holidays. . . .

To my agent, Laurie Liss, for her time and tenacity.

To the entire family of professionals at Dutton Plume, especially to Brian Tart, editor in chief, for his time, patience, and genuine friendship. Besides the editing process, it's always a pleasure.

The Standard

I know something about resilience. For the first twelve years of my life I was subjected to practically every form of continuous physical and psychological torture you could imagine. I should have died. After I was rescued from my alcoholic mother and was fortunate enough to be placed in the care of others, there were a few who boasted that because of my extreme situation I would end up either dead or in prison—the odds against me were insurmountable.

I never saw it that way.

As a child, when my mother stabbed me in the chest, days later I literally crawled on my hands and knees hunting for a wet rag so I could clean my infected wound. At the time I simply applied what I had learned from a first aid class. When my mother refused to feed me for more than ten days, I survived by sneaking water. I did this by swallowing as much as I could from the silver metal ice cube trays whenever I had filled them;

another trick I learned was to suck water from the water basin in the garage. I had to be careful not to turn on the faucet too fast or too slow, for fear that the water pipe might vibrate and alert Mother. When I was thrown in a bathroom with a bucketful of a deadly mixture of ammonia and Clorox that can kill a person in a matter of minutes, I had enough sense to understand that gas rises. All I had to do was stay close to the floor with a wet cloth wrapped around my mouth and nose, praying that the heating vent would come on to circulate fresh air. My relationship with my mother became one of extreme survival. All I had to do was think ahead, believe in myself, and never give up . . . in order to remain alive.

If I learned anything from my unfortunate childhood it is that there is nothing that can dominate or conquer the human spirit. How can you expect to be a good parent, an astute businessperson, or achieve your greatness if you do not focus and harness your inner potential? This is the essence of the message I wish to present to you.

Please understand, this book is not about child abuse. For years I have been mislabeled as "that child abuse guy." I admit I have and I will continue to assist those in the child care fields of awareness and prevention, as well as doing what I can to praise those who give their all to help others in need. After what others have graciously done for me, I feel it is the least I can do. Yet, ever since I was a boy, living at times minute by minute, from the depths of my soul I believed that if I were to live, if I could overcome all that I had suffered, then anything else had to be better. In other words, I learned the value of personal responsibility, resilience, and gratitude. Only, I had to learn at a younger age than most.

When I was a child, Mother did not *allow* me to speak in her house. Period. So at school I would stutter or tremble so badly that kids would tease me, as if I were somehow mentally deficient. Now as an adult, I make a living speaking and I even do comedic storytelling, to the point that I have often been often dubbed "the Robin Williams with Glasses." As a child, because I lived in a garage and never played sports, I had limited coordination. When I was placed in foster care, because of my lack of developmental skills I could not play a simple game of catch, let alone toss a football. Yet years later as a young adult, after a great deal of self-determination, I was fortunate enough to serve my country as an elite aircrew member, entrusted to fly highly classified missions for the United States Air Force. (Can you imagine me passing the psychological examination?) Days after I turned eighteen, I discovered my childhood case had been identified as one of the most severe instances of child abuse in the state of California. And nearly twenty years from the day that I was rescued, I was privileged enough to be selected as one of the Ten Outstanding Young Americans. Other recipients have been President John F. Kennedy, Orson Welles, Anne Bancroft, and my childhood heroes Chuck Yeager and Christopher Reeve.

Please understand, I am not revealing my former experiences to extract sympathy or mentioning my accomplishments for the purpose of feeding my ego. My lovely wife, teenage son, and my higher power keep me grounded. I only offer these examples because, if you are going to spend your precious time and hard-earned money on this book, you should at least be given the decency to know your author's qualifications.

If you want to know the truth, even with all that I've experienced, I still have much to learn. Just like you, I am not perfect. I have problems that I have to address on a daily basis—my self-esteem, being a good husband and father, issues pertaining to my health and my demanding business—which at times can be overwhelming. I simply try to deal with things as best I can. I am not special in any way. I do not possess some magic crystal that contains the secrets of the cosmos. The truth be told: no one has all the answers. There is no such thing as a perfect life. I am simply a regular person who wants to relate to you what I have learned and how you may apply my experiences in your professional and private life. This is my goal.

I mean no disrespect to others in this self-help field who have greater intellect than me, but while there are those who are genuinely sincere in assisting others, there are so many "experts" I know who are full of hot air. I am not a professional "motivational" person. (In fact I hate being called or labeled a "speaker.") I am not a motivational guru, psychic, or New Age "life coach." While I do not have a degree in psychology, I have studied a great deal in this field and have encouraged individuals for over fifteen years with practical, commonsense advice—

ranging from gentle guidance to a psychological kick in the pants.

This book is basically simple and straightforward. I will not attempt to fool you with New Age psychobabble. Yet as simplistic as this book may be, it will be deep rooted on addressing and changing your attitude and behavior. While I pray that this book helps you through the bumps of life, I know it will not solve every problem that suddenly arises. (I wish it could.) For life is ever changing.

Help Yourself is broken down into three separate yet interconnecting sections: 1) Get Rid of the Garbage in Your Life; 2) Know What You Want out of Your Life; and 3) Celebrate Who You Are and What You Have. In their own way, as each chapter deals with specific areas, the underlying meaning will be your own determination to make whatever adjustments you believe necessary as well as a calming sense of appreciation of who you are as a unique individual and what you have accomplished thus far. However, the premise of resilience and gratitude will be more evident in the last two sections. At the end of each chapter I will recap with a few sentences in bold print to help you for future reference.

As you've probably already noticed, I will be speaking directly to you—as if you and I were sitting directly across from each other having a dialogue together. After years assisting others, this is the best way I know how to get my point across. In addition to using some of my experiences as examples throughout this book, I will also provide illustrations from other peoples' lives—some well known to you, others not, but all of whom overcame seemingly impossible odds.

Those who know me know that I loathe writing. I have limited mechanics and it takes me hours to construct a single paragraph. I'd rather visit a dentist to have my teeth extracted without the aid of Novocaine, than spend countless hours on my laptop computer. I am doing this to make a difference. I strongly believe that as a society we some time ago crossed a threshold at which a great number of individuals give up on themselves too easily. We have raised generations who not only look for others to rescue them on virtually every matter concerning their lives, but demand that others—whether parents, friends, employers, or the government—immediately solve their problems to their liking. I learned as a child, shivering in my mother's garage, the value of personal responsibility and opportunity. Where else but America could I be fortunate enough to turn my life around and, more importantly, provide my son with a chance of living a productive, fulfilling life?

In the final analysis, it's up to you. You can read this book or other self-help tomes, watch all the high-energy, all-promising videos, or attend paradise-like weekend retreats, but at the end of the day it is you and you alone who have to make things happen. The cold, hard truth is that outside influences can only propel you so far. The drive has to come from within you. Whether it's this book or anything else you may come in contact with, *you* have to apply what you have learned on a daily basis.

With all of my heart I pray the time we spend together helps you now and for the time to come. I promise you this: I will do my absolute best to provide you with all that I have learned to enable you to live a happier, productive life. This is my standard to you.

Dave Pelzer

Part One

Get Rid of the Garbage in Your Life

1

The Need to Free Yourself

I was too young to know any better. It began between my mother and me around the age of four. By that time, mainly when my father was at work, it was normal for me to walk up to Mother, stand exactly three feet in front of her with my head bent towards the floor, and wait for her to grant me permission to speak, so I could then ask her permission to use the bathroom. I found it strange that my two brothers were permitted to go to the bathroom and do other things that for some reason I was not allowed to do.

I thought the way Mother treated me was completely normal, until one Sunday afternoon, when I was four years old, while father was away, Mother burst into the bedroom, forcing my brothers to scurry for cover, while she proceeded to beat me. By Mother's reddened eyes and foul breath, I knew she was drunk. But because of her intoxicated state, while continuing to hit me Mother slipped, grabbed my left arm to stabilize herself, and fell backward, pulling my arm out of its socket.

When I saw Mother's eyes blink, I knew she, too, had heard and felt the jerk of my arm separating from my shoulder. Yet Mother simply stood up, wiped her hands, shot me a look, then turned and walked away. The next day, the moment Father arrived home from his twenty-four-hour shift at work, Mother suddenly burst into tears, explaining how I had mysteriously fallen from the top bunk. My father, a fireman with medical training, didn't even bat an eye. Neither my brothers nor I ever thought of speaking up.

Hours later, when I received medical attention for the first time since the incident, I knew by the look in the doctor's eyes never to disclose what had really happened. Especially since he rattled on about how kind and sweet my mother was to him and his staff. I remember sitting on a metal swivel chair gazing up at the man in the white jacket, thinking that if everyone likes my mom so much and no one seems concerned about the truth, then *I* must be the problem.

I returned home with my arm in a green sling and a handful of tongue depressors, ready to show off to Father. But I somehow became invisible to him as Mother retold her story again and again. After the drama had reached its peak, I found myself completely alone with Mother. While continuing to cradle me in her arms, she swiveled her head to make sure we were alone. Bending down to look at me, she tightened her grip around me, and the color of her face seemed to darken. Without the need for words the message was clear: *Keep your mouth shut. You tell anyone and next time it will be worse. This will be our little secret.*

It was then, as a four-year-old child raised in the 1960s, that I knew *I was the problem.* I knew I deserved whatever treatment Mother gave me. It was at this age that I learned to push down my feelings of fear and self-worth. It was then that I knew I was alone. Above all, I knew exactly what had happened between Mother and me, but I did not, I could not, do anything to change it.

The Dilemma of Unresolved Issues

Every one of us has a past. All of us have had our share of problems. No one has a perfect life. Loved ones pass away. Parents divorce. Others who don't strive as hard and don't deserve the prized promotion receive it. We've all suffered broken hearts and some, like myself, may have had an unfortunate childhood.

The single most critical element I have found that prevents individuals from achieving their greatness is unresolved issues. It doesn't matter who you are—CEO, single parent, teen, a celebrity, or any other everyday folk—you can never reach your full potential unless you deal with and rid yourself of whatever may be troubling you.

A great number of people who don't deal with problematic situations in their lives develop a tendency to bury their emotions. They may truly believe they've not only addressed the problem but totally dealt with it as well—a short-term solution that may be the answer for some, but in reality rarely solves anything. What they're really doing is developing a bad habit. What's worse is they're still not dealing with the heart of the complication and over time the "quick fix" solution can manifest trouble of its own.

If you find yourself *automatically* reacting, over the simplest thing, in a frustrated, angry, defensive, distant manner, or find yourself trying to escape life by indulging more in your vices than you normally do, it's most likely due to an event linked to a past situation. After years or even weeks of becoming conditioned by the predicament, you may be so used to it that you may not even be aware of *why* you are reacting a particular way. Your mind has become so conditioned, it unconsciously responds as it was taught.

While serving on active duty flying for the air force, I became heavily involved working as a volunteer throughout the state of California with anything having to do with "youth at risk" and those who worked with them. When I received an offer to work part-time at a local juvenile hall, I instantly jumped at the opportunity. Because I was a foster child and had been placed in juvenile hall, I knew what it like for some teens. Yet as many books as I have read and courses I have taken in psychology and human development, I've learned more from the teenagers in juvenile hall than anywhere else.

One young woman, Nancy, had a mouth that would embarrass the most seasoned sailor and at times would spontaneously erupt and assault any boy who might have looked at her the wrong way. One particular time when she exploded, out of fear of her harming herself or others around her, it took three of us adults to restrain this wiry teenager until she finally calmed down. It was because of Nancy's constant negative behavior that she landed in the juvenile detention center. At first, as I'm sure a lot of scared teens do in her condition, Nancy felt she had to *act* a certain way, even more so because of her placement, in order to protect herself and her pride. After a few weeks, Nancy's attitude and behavior worsened to the point that she was facing the possibility of being placed in a psychiatric center.

I, and other staff members with far more experience and education than me, knew Nancy was not as bad as she appeared to be. Without sounding too judgmental, and only after she got to know me, I sincerely asked Nancy, "Why do you act that way?"

"You know why." She shrugged.

Getting to the point I stated, "No, I don't. Why are you *acting* the way you do?"

Nancy's response was so pure it almost knocked me over: "It's all I know."

I was lucky. After other counselors had worked with Nancy for months, she opened up to me, telling me that as a young girl she had constantly been tormented by her brothers and always felt she had to defend herself. As we continued to casually talk back and forth, I chided Nancy by saying, "I don't think anyone's going to even think of messing with you *now*." I emphasized the last word, helping Nancy realize she had yet to break her habit that she had acquired from years ago. "Besides," I added, "if you *act* a certain way, how will others not only judge you, but treat you?"

The staff continued to work with Nancy, helping her to recognize her habitual behavior and replace negative responses with more positive ones. So, when Nancy felt threatened, instead of beating up the boys, she would place her hands on her hips and give them a cold, long stare. Some of the male teens became frightened, unsure what Nancy might do to them; but she was simply controlling herself by counting to ten. Instead of spewing obscenities, Nancy would use her quick wit to fire off a thought-provoking anecdote.

As basic as it sounds, Nancy simply did not wish to be hurt. She felt this way because of a past issue that had taken root. She had *acted tough* for so long that over time she had forgotten why she was acting that *particular* way. In the end, once Nancy became aware, she and she alone had to make the change.

When I think about Nancy's initial statement, "It's all I know," it reminds me of something Oprah Winfrey once said on her show when she consoled a young lady with low self-esteem who found herself in trouble as well: "Now that you know better, do better."

A lot of folks harbor portions of their past in their hearts until it hardens and develops as a "reflex" type of response, until the behavior and/or attitude becomes normal for them.

Letting Go

All of us tend to suppress problems rather than deal with them as soon as they unexpectedly "pop up." And it doesn't have to be from some traumatic experience either. Teens and adults, especially those with low esteem, who crave independence and have the tremendous desire to belong, will do anything to fit in. Do you know anyone who's felt slightly intimidated attending college or being the "new guy" at work, and has kept his opinions to himself for fear of making a statement that might appear stupid or antagonistic? There are some of us, including myself, who have been in turbulent relationships and stayed in them, and would rather just go along than to risk being abandoned or face the possibility of a confrontation.

All of us at one time or another have found ourselves in uncomfortable conditions that we did not deal with. Again, it may be because of a habit from our past. I believe if we learn to deal with the everyday problems of life, it helps us all the more when something more arduous comes along.

Let's say you're at work, counting the minutes before you can bolt from the office. You've been looking forward to the weekend—to be with your family or have some quiet time by yourself—ever since Monday when you first rolled out of that warm, comfortable bed. You've been swamped this entire week and because you are so dedicated to your job, you've put off your personal needs. But now, seconds before you grab your things and flee, in strolls your boss. He's a huge, overbearing blowhard with the breath of an ox. With sweat trickling down his brow, he dumps a stack of reports that require your instant attention. With a wave of his hand he apologizes, for he would have gotten them to you sooner but he was out playing a round of golf. "Either way," he demands, "you've got to take care of this."

"But I'm about to leave; I've got plans!" you plead.

"That's okay," your boss replies as he leaves your cubicle, "I don't mind. Just make sure it's all done and ready for me first thing Monday morning."

You're fuming. Your heart rate quickens, your body becomes tense. You want to give your boss a piece of your mind, a spray can of deodorant, and a case of Altoids. On the drive home all you can think about is that man. Suddenly, you're stuck in traffic. The air conditioner is on the fritz. You miss your exit. Then you run out of gas because you were thinking about work when you passed the gas station. You're the poster child for Murphy's Law: If it can get worse, it will.

While I mean no disrespect to those in management and while the preceding is simply an illustration, I've known people who have had that type of experience. But answer this: With all that frustration, what kind of weekend are you going to have? Probably not a good one. In the preceding story, unless you quit, the only way out is to complete the task as best as you can and as quickly as possible so as to spend the remainder of your time on your terms.

In reality, have you ever had a similar overbearing problem that stemmed from work, a different kind of situation at home, or a more personal matter that, not dealt with, became so overwhelming that you became consumed by the situation, to the point it affected your attitude and every aspect of your day? I have. Have your problems affected your sleep, to the point that you could not get the rest you needed because of your bad day, then got up feeling groggy, unfocused, and still consumed by that troubling issue?

The Need to Rest Your Mind

So why is it that you can't get your mind to let go? The basic answer is your brain is simply trying to find the precise solution to that particular problem. If the problem is overwhelming, your mind will not function to its full capacity because it is being drawn to the dilemma it is focused on. If you find yourself constantly losing sleep, this is a serious predicament. If the brain is not allowed to rest it can, psychologically speaking, crash.

When it comes to the importance of resting one's mind, I recall a time years ago while I was serving in the military. I had the rare opportunity to observe one of the army's elite organizations, the Rangers, during the last phase of their training. Having been a graduate of the army's paratrooper jump school, I appreciate and respect how grueling and rigorous their qualifications are. These razor-sharp commandos working in small units are hardened to accomplish their objective at all costs and against all odds. Since the last part of the Rangers' training is under constant, intense conditions of simulated combat, the trainees are required to complete their various tasks while being physically and psychologically pushed and pulled in every direction, with only one hour's sleep a day.

Imagine yourself wearing the same set of clothes for over a week, chilled to the bone, past exhaustion, muscles aching from being weighed down by your weapon, ammunition, and forty-pound backpack, and all the while you're crawling, hiking, rappelling, or rafting with not only simulated mortars exploding wherever you step and gunfire rattling off, but a mock force that wishes you harm. Yet, as physically tired as these men were, their reflexes remained razor sharp and their morale was extremely high. To answer the question how in the world these men were able to do it, a veteran instructor smiled, stating, "These men are in top physical and, more importantly, psychological condition. The brain only needs thirty to forty minutes of sound sleep a day to recharge itself. It's like resetting a circuit breaker. We bombard these men with ever-changing, life-threatening scenarios, so when they sleep, they sleep well. By the time they wake up, their brains are rested and ready to go.

"They have to adjust quickly, effectually. They cannot allow anything to get into their minds that may bog them down. This entire course is more psychological than physical. If your mind's not rested, focused, or if you tell yourself you ain't gonna make it, you're history, you're washed out of the program. The body can endure practically anything—pain, fatigue, you name it—*but it's the mind that matters."*

I think of my experience with the Rangers as a hard-core business-management course. Those professionals are able to work through a multitude of situations and are able to do so, in part because they allow their minds to rest. The main lesson I learned, which I use to this day, is no matter the situation anyone may be facing, the brain has to shut down or "reset" itself every day, in order to deal with the challenges of the next day.

I'm in no way saying you have to be some he-man Rambo commando in order to sort through your issues. Truth be told, I'm a wimp compared to those in uniform. I'm middle aged, too lazy, and no longer do three hundred sit-ups a day. But I know this: With all that every one of us does in a single day, with all the problems that bombard us, if we do not learn to deal with these issues and turn off "the switch," we will run ourselves into the ground.

The reason why you may not be able to get a good night's sleep is your mind is desperately searching for an answer to your problem. Look at it this way: Your brain is like a CD-ROM—it is constantly spinning at extreme speeds in its function to keep the machine, your body, operating. The brain not only processes information but stores data faster and better than any computer chip mankind can devise. If you have "programmed" your brain not to address a situation, your "computer" in a way will store your problems in its "To be solved at a later date" file; but over time when that file becomes full, the CD-ROM becomes task saturated, continuing to spin as it searches for a solution to its function. So what can eventually happen? The computer crashes.

This is why I cannot stress enough the value of a good night's sleep. With a recharged battery you are all the better when it comes to tackling whatever comes your way. When it comes to dealing with issues, think of it as removing data from your computer disk that you need to do on a daily basis, so your file does not become too full, forcing your computer to crash.

You need to reprogram how you deal with troubling issues, just as Nancy did when she became upset, by replacing a bad program with a more positive one. Imagine being the president of the United States. Every single day the president is bombarded by countless situations, up to life-threatening crises, that can have repercussions around the world. How does the president do it? The president does not have superhero powers with Einsteinian intelligence, but is a human being just like you and me. And like any good manager, the president deals with any situation by confronting it. After collecting all the information, the president considers all the options and consequences of each scenario, makes a decision, and moves on to the next problem. Not to downplay the magnitude of the office of the president, but it is basically what most of us do on a daily basis—from single parents balancing their budget, those who apply themselves every day at work, to students trying to remain focused when studying for final exams.

So, when a situation arises, address *your problem*, consider *your options*, then accept the repercussions of *your decision*. If you believe in spiritual guidance, meditate or pray about it, *then* make *your decision* and let the situation go. After you've made your decision it is vital that you relax, just as the president plays a round of golf in the middle of a crisis so that his mind can unwind and can focus on the next series of situations. And you, just like the president, will find that once a problem is solved another one quickly replaces it. But over time as you learn to continually deal with problems, however frustrating or disgusting they may be, you'll discover that not only will your esteem grow because now you're in charge of your life—and not some ghost from your past keeping you down—but more important, psychologically you will be all the healthier.

Controlled Eruptions

Please understand: you will never be able to solve all your problems to your liking. And at times you will feel overwhelmed and frustrated. That's life. Remember that story about the pompous boss with the bad breath? You know you can't tell him off, and you will most likely have to give up another weekend to ensure the job is done. Yet, inside of you this enormous pressure is building up like a volcano. What can you do? Two words: *controlled eruptions.*

We now realize how damaging it is to keep everything bottled up, so we have to relieve that pressure. Years ago my son, Stephen, was playing Little League baseball. As much as he tried, he simply was not playing one of his best games. Inning after inning I could tell by his body language that the strain was building up inside of him. On the drive home Stephen was like a statue; he refused to talk and barely moved. As a parent I believe in being a positive role model and instilling manners. However, Stephen and I have always had an agreement that when a situation dictated I would, for just a few minutes, not grade him as my son but as his friend. This was one of those times. I told Stephen that for the next five minutes he could kick, yell, swear, or basically do whatever he had to, to get the tension out of his system. After a few seconds of hesitation, Stephen purged. Five minutes later he collected himself, then we talked a bit more and within a few miles he felt better. Keep in mind it didn't change the outcome of his game. But by opening up, Stephen was able to think about what to do *the next time* he might be in that same position, and by relieving that pressure he felt different than he had immediately after his game.

Stephen basically addressed the situation, made a decision on what to do next time, and moved on.

Opening up not only helps you relieve that pent-up

anxiety, but sometimes can be just enough to get you through.

You can do the same thing Stephen did. Having a bad day at work? Or on your way to work or school after a problem at home? And, to make matters worse, is it a big day for you and you only have little time between where you've been and where you're going? If you have to, and if you have no other way of relieving the strain, during the drive to your destination allot yourself a specific amount of time to vent a little and shout in the car. Smack that steering wheel a few times. Screech at that radio talk-show host. Imagine that your supervisor or that person who made you upset is beside you and give that person a piece of your mind. Within reason, alleviate some of that pressure to clear your mind and enable it to focus on the events of your day.

Do not get so upset that you cause an accident. Again, I stress the term *controlled eruptions. You are in control* as you *vent that pressure.* Sometimes when I'm driving, I bark at the radio for a few minutes until I feel better. When I'm alone, looking at photos of my wife and son, realizing they are the reason I do what I do is enough to pull me through. Before or after a big day I work out at the gym. At home I'll walk for hours among the redwood trees. No matter my hectic schedule, *every day* I try to do something that will alleviate the stress of my day. My wife, Marsha: she shops. She has a weakness for makeup, shoes, and anything within the confines of a mall. But at least Marsha comes home happier than when she left, and proudly proclaims her mantra "I feel much better!"

On a more serious note, by leaving the office Marsha gets away from her pressure-filled environment. In her car Marsha applies that time to decompress as she sings out loud. In a psychological sense, walking the length of the mall several times at a brisk pace helps Marsha diminish her stress all the more. The point I'm trying to make is: within reason do what you have to in order to relieve your daily stress. Take some form of control—get away from that confrontation, write a scathing letter that you never mail, take a stroll anywhere you feel at peace. Once a day, three times a day, a hundred times a day, whatever it takes, make a sincere effort to deal with life's unpleasantries as best as you can.

Once, when I was speaking for a business and after hearing how the morale was low and production was down, I recommended that the organization dispose of office rank and have a productive gripe session. Without the fear of reprisal, anyone would be allowed to speak her mind, not only on what was wrong, but she had to have a recommendation to make things better. In this way, those who were preoccupied not only addressed their problems once and for all, but became proactive in the process. The only stipulations I made were that the discussion not be a onetime quick fix, but should at least be a quarterly conference or when the situation warranted; and secondly, it was not an opportunity to be used as a perpetual whine fest. As time went on, morale and productivity rose while stress, apprehensiveness, and needless complaining declined.

This is basically the same method that Stephen and I used after his troublesome ball game, as well as do a lot of families. Every so often dispense with the protocol, speak your mind freely, openly or to yourself, and do something about the complication. By addressing and relieving pressure you are helping to ensure that the circuit breaker in your head can be reset, so you can live your life better.

Cleansing Your Soul

However, on the other side of the coin, I cannot tell you how many people I have met who have become helpless victims or jaded souls. Why? They either became too frightened of opening up or allowed their unresolved issues to get the best of them. Even though some of these individuals fully realized, through their own choice, they were destined to live a joyless life, the prospect of dealing with their problematic situation became too much for them. The sad reality is that if some of these people could have confronted the problem they would have seen the situation for *what it was*, rather than *what they thought it was*, and they might have turned the tide.

To use my son as another example, when Stephen was about five years old I could tell something was troubling him. Whenever I had tried to get him to talk about it, he simply blushed with embarrassment, saying I wouldn't understand. Finally, for whatever reason, I was able to get

Stephen to talk. At first he was a little apprehensive. He even stopped before he got to the core of the issue and wanted to run off. Thankfully, as he plowed through, his eyes suddenly widened with the discovery that his problem was not as bad as he had thought it was. The second Stephen finished, he sat amazed at his own breakthrough of simply opening up and telling me everything, and before I could give him any fatherly advice he kissed me and ran off to spend the rest of his day playing outside.

When I listen to folks who tell me their predicaments, I try to get them to open up, to tell me everything, rather than scratch the surface. For the most part, when we get to the core of the issue, we realize the situation that we held on to for so long, that caused us so much pain, is not as bad as it seems or seemed at the time.

For lack of a better word, it's what I call *purging*. When you have stomach troubles, and if they're bad enough, your body will physically reject whatever it is that is making you sick. Often when I have been sick, I did not physically regurgitate everything I should have, so I remained in great pain until I purged whatever it was that made me feel ill. Then, like a lot of people, within a short time I actually felt better. The reason: There was nothing left within me to make me sick.

I am not trying to sound tasteless, but I cannot tell you how important, how imperative, it is for you to *psychologically purge* yourself of whatever is ailing you. After everything you have read thus far, if you still have situations that seem to pull you down or if you seem tied to something in your past, if you do not "vomit" from the recesses of your soul, you are most likely destined to be a slave of your experience.

Have you ever known someone who has been in therapy for years? Now, I am not taking a jab at those in the field of psychology, but one of the reasons a person may feel she needs that much help may be because she is still skating around the edges, rather than getting to the core of the issue that required her to be in therapy in the first place.

* * *

I have had the privilege of meeting hundreds of thousands of people, and I have seen so many lives that were crushed because some kept issues locked away deep in their hearts. But once they purged, and I mean released everything, at the very least they felt a little alleviated, cleaner. Their lives' perspective changed for the better. Overall they became more self-reliant and independent. Over time they became whole. Like everyone else, these folks still had to deal with everyday situations, but having freed themselves from their shackled past they were able to do so now with a little more relative ease.

To reiterate, I am not talking about a troubled childhood. Divorce, losing a love, a career that might have been, violated trust . . . you name it, all of us have endured the deepest of pain. But are you a prisoner to your past or stronger and wiser because of it?

Yes, purging yourself can be painful, embarrassing, and at times disgusting. What other options do you have? Ask yourself this: *If what I've been doing so far isn't working, isn't it about time I did something different?*

Years ago Bob, a dear friend of mine, lost his father to cancer. Three years after the death of his father, Bob still grieved over his loss. Over time he became reclusive, overweight, and miserable. It affected Bob's marriage, the relationship with his children, his promising career, his sleep, and ultimately his health. On one visit, because he had known me for years, Bob allowed me to take him out for a drive. Without his knowing our destination, I drove him to the cemetery. Once there, I had to pry him from the car and lead him to his father's tombstone, where he sheepishly stood until suddenly his body shook, then he exploded with a surge of tears. While a grown man weeping on his hands and knees in the middle of the day might prove unmasculine and embarrassing to some, Bob later confessed not only how cleansed he felt, but how an invisible weight—that had held him down for years—lifted from his soul.

For years Bob had carried in his heart the regret that he'd never had the opportunity to say good-bye to his father. Bob also lived with the guilty sense that he could have been a better son. That evening back at home Bob finally fell into a deep, sound sleep. With every day afterward he made progress. While he informed me he would never be the *same*, he has now dedicated himself to being a *better* person and a more loving father to his children.

It had taken Bob three years and an endless amount of

suffering for him to finally come face to face with his issue. His upbeat outlook didn't come overnight, and it took him several more "talks" with his father until he felt strong enough to shed himself of guilt and of whatever baggage he had carried with him for so long.

Bob's situation changed when he achieved a sense of closure with his father. He was able to open up at his father's grave site. For others, I recommend talking to someone, anyone. Sometimes it just takes that one person whom you know to make the difference—a parent, spouse, lover, friend, someone at work. As long as you feel comfortable and trust that person, I recommend you take the chance. For folks with more serious issues, I recommend professional help—counselor, therapist, psychologist, someone who specializes in that particular field—which can help guide you along the path to becoming a more wholesome, fulfilled, happy person.

Again—if what you are doing so far isn't working, isn't it about time you did something different? Make the change to free yourself!

HELP YOURSELF REMINDERS

* SETTLE YOUR PROBLEMS AS PROMPTLY AND AS THOROUGHLY AS YOU ARE ABLE.
* LET GO OF A PAST YOU CANNOT CHANGE.
* IN THE MIDST OF FIGHTING LIFE'S BATTLES, RELAX.

* VENT YOUR FRUSTRATIONS IN A CONTROLLED YET CLEANSING MANNER.

* HAVE THE COURAGE TO PURIFY YOURSELF OF WHATEVER MAY BE HOLDING YOU BACK.

2

Surviving a Negative Environment

Recently I read an article about a confessed killer's defense attorney who pleaded for the court's mercy. The attorney claimed that his defendant, "Mr. Smith," was simply a victim of society. Since Mr. Smith had no father figure, his mother became an unwilling slave to drugs, and as a teenager Mr. Smith could not adapt to the stringent guidelines of school, so he fell in with the wrong crowd. His only role models were from television, violent movies, and graphic video games. If there was an injustice, the attorney ranted, it was against Mr. Smith. The attorney was then reported to have lowered his voice and, dipping his head toward the jury that would decide on his client's fate, sighed, "My client is simply a product of a negative environment."

With all due respect to the Mr. Smiths of the world, being exposed to a negative setting *does not* mean you are either destined for a life of crime or doomed to an unfulfilled life. Former chairman of the Joint Chiefs of Staff

General Colin Powell, the first African American to hold such office, was raised in a rat-infested ghetto in Harlem, New York. His parents—immigrants from Jamaica—did all they could for their son, yet it was Colin who had to decide his fate. Some may say it would have been understandable for young Colin to have been swallowed up by the gritty streets of New York or fallen through the cracks of society, but he, wanting something more for himself, enlisted in the army, immersed himself in college, and eventually came up through the ranks to lead America's armed forces in operations Desert Shield and Desert Storm.

As previously addressed in the last chapter, all of us have had unpleasant experiences and situations that we have had to deal with on a daily basis. And, many of us have been subjected to bad surroundings. Again, it comes down to awareness. While both Mr. Smith and General Powell experienced unfortunate conditions, in my estimation both individuals made vastly different choices that drastically affected their futures. No matter the environment, there comes a time when the choice is ours.

When I was removed from my mother's custody and became a ward of the court through the foster-care system, I was required to meet with a psychiatrist. One time the doctor had a private meeting with my foster mother and informed her that, in his professional opinion, because of my extended exposure to a violent and desperate world, there was little hope of my becoming "normally adjusted." And he believed that since the law of averages was against me, I would most likely end up in prison or would commit suicide.

But what if we, like Colin Powell, used our negative environment to make us strive for something better?

Because of my childhood experience, all I desired was a better life for myself. From generations ago to this very day, countless individuals who have lived under oppressive conditions have made the journey to America, to have an opportunity to make a life for themselves and their children. These individuals took a gamble and faced whatever obstacles were in their way and paid whatever price they had to pay in order to change their setting. And once they arrived, things did not get better overnight. The bottom line: Our country's bedrock is one man or woman with a resilient, self-reliant attitude. While adverse surroundings play an important role in our lives, if we are willing we do not have to be dominated by them.

That is why when I hear or read a story of a Mr. Smith and how his dismal surroundings *forced* him to harm others, I become slightly agitated. Through a choice of his own, Mr. Smith used his past environment as a crutch. And no matter one's environment, that does not give a person the excuse to promote chaos and inflict harm on others.

To be fair, I must say I have been told that by the time children reach ten years of age, their environment does have a significant bearing on their lives—their esteem, prejudices, limitations, how they view the world, and how they fit into it. However, from all the reports I have read and the specialists I know in the field of human behavior, I strongly believe: if people have a basic understanding of right from wrong, possess a strong desire to better themselves and persist in their cause, they can break the chain of a negative environment.

A Matter of Choice

But even with the best of surroundings, *it is the individual who decides his or her own fate*. Years ago as a foster child, I had a close friend who came from the epitome of the perfect family. My friend Joe had two loving parents, who both worked hard and were active in church, and their neighborhood resembled something out of *Leave It to Beaver*. Joe seemingly had everything. With Joe's passion for science fiction and space exploration, we all knew he was destined to work with NASA. But some anomaly happened to Joe during his teenage years—an issue he refused to address with even his closet friends and family—and to this day Joe, even with the support that I would have killed for when I was a kid, has a fraction of the ambition he once had and his dreams are a thing of the past. As sad as it is for me to say, Joe, even with a positive environment and guidance, lost his desire, and the loss affects him still.

When it comes to dealing with negative surroundings, I believe it boils down to three options: We become a product of a negative environment; we find a way out of the environment; or adjust to it as best we can.

Mr. Smith is the perfect example of a person's becoming the product of a negative environment. I believe that all of us carry portions of our past throughout our lives. But even a bad experience doesn't have to be detrimental. My mother, before she began treating me so inhumanely, would always decorate the entire house with Christmas ornaments the day after Thanksgiving. Now, every year, the day following Thanksgiving, my family and I break open the boxes of ornaments, hang the bright lights, and adorn our home as my mother once did. With all that Mother did to me, remembering some of the good times helps me to let go of the bad ones.

When You Can't Let Go of Your Past

But some people who can't seem to let go of their negative past may find themselves doomed because of it. A woman whom I have known for years, Nora, had a tough childhood and was constantly berated by her mother, who either lied to Nora over the smallest things or made reflexive excuses, blaming her problems on her daughter. One day, as a teenager, Nora ran away, so no one could "control her" or "tell her what to do" any longer. That was over twenty-five years ago, and to this day whenever a serious or everyday situation needs to be addressed, Nora psychologically runs away. She either brushes off the predicament, instantaneously fires off a veil-thin lie, or blames her woes on someone else. As an adult she has become a carbon copy of her mother, to the point that Nora, who still loathes her mother's behavior toward her, has moved away several times to begin anew, but within weeks has always returned to be near her. And Nora, who hates her mother's meddling in her everyday affairs, calls her mother several times a day seeking her approval. At times Nora, who has the tremendous capacity for kindness and could achieve her greatness, lacks the resolve to break away from her environment.

I have the highest respect for anyone who gives her all to better herself, for I know from personal experience how arduous it can be to break away from a controlling situation. That's why it's hard for me to tell Nora's story. I saw so much within her; if she could only have dealt with her issues and "broken away" once and for all, I believe with all my heart that Nora would have been a happier more fulfilled person.

When it comes to breaking away from a negative environment, sometimes we have to do just that, and as hard and as emotional as it may be, we have to make a clean break. When folks tell me that they absolutely cannot, for whatever reason, get along with that one person, to the point that the relationship consists of yelling or tempers constantly erupting like a volcano, then my advice is: Stay away. There is practically no reason why someone has to expose himself to that setting. Maintain your distance from that family member, lover, friend, or those at work. If things are that bad, for now, at least, there's no need to complicate or ignite the situation further, for it can only pull you in deeper. And if you have to attend those family reunions, social events, or meetings at work, keep your cool and limit your exposure. On behavioral matters, if you find yourself saying things or acting in ways you normally never did before, it may be because of your negative surroundings. Sure, that one person or that group may supposedly accept you or be nice to you, but ask yourself this: Do you really like the person you are becoming? If not, then break away and stay away.

Maybe for Nora and others like her, the "pull" from her environment was too much for them to deal with. I'm not sure if we can even appreciate how much our everyday environment may have an affect on us. Have you known anyone who has tried to quit smoking but had friends who constantly smoked? It's nearly impossible unless he makes a drastic change. The same goes for those who are addicted to drugs or alcohol, or fight to keep their emotions under control. While serving in the air force and volunteering to work with those in prison and juvenile hall, I found that as much as the inmates wanted to change their lives, without hesitation nearly all of them, when finally released, went back to the same setting and eventually "cycled" by reacting as they had before . . . and were returned to be incarcerated again.

The refusal either to stay away or break away once and for all from such a detrimental setting could possibly—just as with those who "cycle" in and out of institutions—lead to serious consequences. One can never tell if suddenly one day they will find themselves "sucked in" and by the time they realize their situation discover it is too late to escape. For some folks who are already neck deep in their environment, over time it becomes part of their psychological makeup. Are you familiar with the fable about the coyote and the scorpion? Being stranded on one side of the river and wanting to cross, the scorpion tried to convince the coyote to carry him across the water. "But if I do, surely you will sting me with your deadly tail," stated the coyote. "No, I promise, I will not," guaranteed the scorpion. So the coyote allowed the scorpion to crawl on his back and began to make his way across the river. All went well until they reached the middle of the stream when suddenly the coyote felt a sharp sting behind his head. "Why did you do that?" the coyote cried. "By doing so you realize both of us are now doomed to die!" "Yes," replied the deadly creature, "I am fully aware. But I could not help myself. It's in my nature!"

My point is be extremely careful of where you "tread" and the types of people you may "pick up along the way" during the course of your life.

The Baggage of Guilt

From what I know, those who try to break away from a negative environment may carry with them either guilt or a form of appeasement or combination of both, making it all the harder to break free. Even with the fantastic life I am able to live today, at times I feel a wall of shame crash over me like a wave. There are instances when my hands shake, I stutter, and parts of my body lock up. When I was rescued, my brothers still had to endure my mother's insanity, while I was being nurtured and protected by my foster parents. Today, I focus on applying myself to help others so they will not have to suffer the same treatment as my brothers and I did.

I'm not the only one who has to deal with the burden of guilt. A few years ago I had the honor of meeting a woman named Michelle, who is a survivor of the Holocaust. When she was a child, toward the end of World War II in Europe, the Nazis put Michelle and her mother on a train that was to be sent to a death camp. Michelle's mother gave her life to save her young daughter Michelle. When I had the opportunity to speak with Michelle, she revealed a crushing force that had weighed upon her all of her life. "Why was I spared when so many others died?" After she poured out her feelings, I held her and asked her the question "Was there anything you could have done to prevent what had happened?" Michelle shook her head no. "Then you can do no more."

I think all of us in one way or another carry a regret that's connected to our circumstances. As stressed in the last chapter: In order to move forward one has to let go. When I was being consoled as a teenager in foster care for the immense guilt and shame I felt at the time, as I was desperately trying the find the precise answers to the conflict between Mother and me, the therapist asked a bold question: "Is there anything you can do to change the past?" I sobbed, shaking my head no. "Then you can do no more!" My therapist instructed, "Learn from it and move forward."

As simplistically obvious as this may sound, none of

us has the capability to step into a time machine and transport ourselves to the past and change the one single event or element in our lives that would have made things right. Even if you could, I believe—as in the case with my mother and me—that it was in fact a *small series of events* that led to our situation. If I were sitting with you right now I would simply say, "Learn from your past! Don't become a prisoner of it!"

If you feel guilty because you were the cause of what may have happened, again learn from the situation, and resolve not to repeat the same mistake. Unfortunately, there are a great number of people who make the same errors over and over again, in part because of their environment. Just over a year ago I remarried. Because my first marriage failed, I am now more determined to work daily on my relationship with my wife. All of us have regrets and I'm sure we have said and done things we are not proud of. If you find yourself unable to move forward or feel "pulled in" because of your past environment, ask yourself: *Was there anything I could have done to prevent the situation?* If the answer is yes, then *do* something different now and become a better person because of it. If your response is no, then you have your answer. Next, ask yourself: *Did I do the best I could at the time?* If the answer is yes, then let the past go. If the response is no, again, learn something from it and *do* something positive about the situation the next time.

When it comes to breaking the chains of a negative environment, I think of my eldest brother, Ron, who has been a police officer for nearly twenty-five years. Ron, like countless others, including Mr. Smith and Nora, could have been pulled down because of his negative environment. However, as if in response to it Ron has applied himself to serving and protecting others. I have found that a great number of those who work in the law-enforcement, social-services, and foster-care fields do so because of their unfortunate environment. Part of the reason I do what I do is so I can assist others to break free as well.

Pop star legend and super diva Tina Turner is another example. After surviving years of an abusive marriage to a controlling, drug-addicted husband, Ms. Turner summoned the strength and guts needed to literally crawl away from her environment. Afterward, and with overwhelming odds, this lady gave everything she had—physically, emotionally, and spiritually—for the mere chance of recapturing the career she so desperately loved. But because Ms. Turner did what she had to in order to free herself, she was able to achieve the phenomenal career that she maintains to this day.

Those Who Appease

Making sure you don't become a prisoner to a negative environment also means being careful that you don't become a "please-aholic." So many folks, myself included, who are or were exposed to a negative setting, with or without knowing may find themselves overcompensating by trying to obtain other people's approval—parents, relatives, friends, spouses, coworkers, etc.—especially those who make them feel inferior. As a child, when my mother constantly berated me for being stupid, I tried to compensate for her affection. Without the aid of glasses I would read mammoth-sized books in a dark garage. Months later, when I brought home good grades on my report card, Mother would beat me because she claimed she was still disappointed with me. But even after the next report card, when I proudly displayed to Mother the highest marks, she still wasn't satisfied. No matter how many chores I flawlessly accomplished, no matter how hard I strove as a child to be perfect for her, nothing I did made Mother love me.

Years later as a teenager in foster care, because I was so desperate to make friends at school I made myself into the class goof and soon became the butt of everyone's jokes. When I was approached by a group of kids who were *thinking* about being my friends, craving their approval I began stealing candy bars, then toys and records, for my newfound "friends." As you can guess, sad to say in the end, after I gave all of myself, no one liked me or wanted anything to do with me.

As an adult I realized I was still trying to please others too much when it came to business matters. At times I was fully aware that I was getting walked on, taken advantage of, or was doing more and going to more extremes than others. When I discovered that as an author and speaker I was "mismanaged," I asked, "Why? After all I've done, why? Why me?" The responses were that I was such a nice guy, no one ever thought I would say anything. My overwhelming need to please kept me from standing up for myself.

Just a few years ago, out of habit I found myself practically begging one of my relatives to attend a prestigious award ceremony in which I had been selected as one of the Ten Outstanding Young Americans. Because my esteem was so low, not only did I not feel worthy of the recognition, but with every word that spilled from my mouth I found myself promising my relative the moon, while inside I knew I was making a complete jerk out of myself. Even as I hung up the phone, I thought if I could only do this *one thing* or maybe if I did or said *something else,* then I might be worthy of the attention and respect of a family member who had never truly cared about me in the first place! For most of my life, my desire to please others was so powerful that I instantly did so without a second thought for myself.

Please don't get me wrong: I think it's important for all of us to apply ourselves, with everything we have, every day, but we need to channel our efforts for the right cause. And while I believe it's vital for all of us to be kind and display manners while being humble, I have learned the valuable lesson of doing so *without* giving myself away in the process. Because of my initial environment, grappling for others' approval was all I knew. For people like my mother, my fair-weather friends, or the inconsiderate people I worked with as an adult, I could have discovered the cure for cancer, AIDS, *and* the common cold, but, alas, it would not have been enough to make anyone like me for who I was.

I'm only suggesting that you be careful of being a please-aholic. The truth is, no matter what you do for the sole purpose of having others admire you, your efforts, as mine were, will most likely be in vain. And no matter how much you do for others—those so-called "friends"—it can never be enough. You may be liked by others for a while, but only as long as you have something they want from you. How many stories have you read about movie stars or rock stars who are suddenly surrounded by so many so-called "friends," right up until the moment their fame or money runs out?

Remember that, as much as Nora detested her mother, she would still desperately crave her approval? It seems to me that there are people who feed, in a sense, off of others. These people are not happy in their lives, for whatever reason (most likely an unresolved issue from their past) and keep drawing from the well of others to fill whatever ails them. No matter how much they suck off of others, no matter how miserable they can make others in order to elevate their own self-worth . . . it is never enough!

Resolve to Take a Stand

There can be endless reasons why folks may not like us, no matter what we do. Without any feelings of revenge or animosity, I truly believe my mother basically hated herself, *then* the world around her. Unfortunately, Mother took her frustrations out on me, my brothers, and anyone else she believed got in her way. As a teenager in foster care, my "friends" at school never liked me, but fed off my desperation for companionship, that enabled them to lead me on. Those I worked with may have thought I was too naive or lacked the guts to stand up for myself. As for my relative whom I pleaded with to attend the ceremony with me, his refusal may have been the result either of resentment that I was to receive an accolade or of shame at what had happened to me as a child. In the final analysis, does it really matter? I cannot tell you how many hours I have wasted dissecting the hows or whys and what I could have done for the sole result of appeasing others. In the end, you must have the will to simply be yourself.

My pivotal moment came minutes after my father's funeral. Just days before, my father had passed away in my arms, as a lonely broken man who could not even say good-bye with mere words or a blink of his eyes due to the severity of his cancer. In the months that Father lay in the hospital bed, Mother never made the ten-mile drive to see him. Immediately after the service, beside the church, in a fit of rage Mother exploded at me, slapping me on the side of my face so that a trickle of blood fell to the pavement. As she raised her hand to strike me again, I surprised myself by saying, "Don't even think about it! All those years you tried to break me and I'm still here. I'm a good person. I try my best in everything I set out to do. I make mistakes, I screw up, but I learn. I don't blame others for my problems. I stand on my own. I won't waste my life away. If you taught me *anything*, you taught me that."

That was a crucial juncture for me. I never planned it, and I never meant to be arrogant, but as I spoke those words I could feel a giant weight lift from my shoulders. Those few moments in time set my life on a different course. I didn't have to repeat the cycle of hate and self-destruction that I had been exposed to. And no matter my past, I had just made my declaration to break away from a sickening environment.

Now, after a few hard knocks, I stand up for myself. I ask the hard questions. Without being arrogant or rude, I'll speak my piece. Every day I do my best and if there are those who disagree with me, it's not the end of the world. I no longer beat myself up in the vain hope of others' consent. At times it's a hard balancing act, but I keep myself in constant check. I can do no more.

My recommendation is not to waste your time and energy. There are far more important things in life. When you please others in the hopes of being accepted, you lose your self-worth in the process. As elementary as this sounds: To help yourself, you have to be yourself. Be the best person you can possibly be. When you make a mistake or feel beaten down, learn from the situation and pick yourself up. The folks you may be trying to impress, if they like what they see, will most likely come to you. And instead, you can apply your time and efforts in a different direction, in favor of others in need who could benefit from your unique qualities and sincerity.

By being more self-assured, you're not only taking a

stand but you will actually learn more quickly to adapt to a negative environment.

It's Not All Bad

Basically, we all know what to do when it comes to our environment, and if the world were perfect we wouldn't have to give it a second thought. The reality is that the world we live in isn't perfect and we are only human, prey to our emotions; even though at times we know what we may be doing isn't the best thing for us, especially when it comes to matters of the heart. And since there is so much that can pull us down and because we are constantly bombarded by negativity, all I am trying to suggest is for you to lessen your exposure to a negative environment. Even though parents continually remind their children and teenagers of the importance of this admonition—ranging anywhere from whom they hang out with, whom they date, and whom to stay away from—a large number of adults I have met believe that *they* are impervious to their environment.

Have you noticed at work that the smallest amount of negativity can erode or even paralyze someone's home or business? Personality conflicts, political agendas, or feelings of revenge become the main focus. The negativity takes your mind off your objective, your everyday activities, your studies, or your work, and you become caught up in something that doesn't really matter. On the personal side, I'm sure we all know someone who hates the idea of family reunions or being with friends of friends who are so strange that they must be from another planet. At work, have you ever seen or heard those at the "water cooler club"? A small band of whiners, conspirators, gossipers, whose work output is marginal at best, who know who's been doing what to whom and for how long.

What do you do? Since we will never be able to change everything in our world to our liking, we have to learn to adjust and make the most of what we have. The one thing I have been told is that the key to a good marriage, whether it is one of business or a personal union, is *compromise*. When it comes to surviving a negative environment you can at least begin by limiting your exposure. Think of it as radiation: a sudden burst of exposure can instantly vaporize you, but what a lot of people forget is that small continual doses of radiation can be just as deadly. So, limit your *exposure* to a negative environment. If possible stay the heck away from those water cooler gossipers, the folks craving your appeasement, or anyone or group that you don't *have to* put up with. And whenever you come into contact with those people or situations that drive you up the wall, be the better person and make the best of things. Grit your teeth, and smile, smile, smile.

For my second deployment to Saudi Arabia, I left behind my four-year-old son days before Christmas of 1990. I was fully aware of the high probability of fighting a war against Saddam Hussein and all the elements that went with it. I could have complained how unfair the situation was, whined about lack of creature comforts that I and the other five hundred thousand men and women did not have due to our location in the desert, but the only thing it would have accomplished would be to take my mind off my assigned mission. There was not one thing I could have done to change my environment, so to make things a little bit better I brought with me several freshly cut Christmas trees that were so huge I could barely fit them into the airplane, stockings with candies, and a few cases of apple cider. Others brought small CD players with Christmas music. On Christmas day the celebration only lasted a few minutes. And it didn't change the stress and anxiety we were dealing with daily, but it did make matters just a little bit better. I believe that sometimes these small things might be just enough to get you through.

So many folks complain about things without dealing with their circumstances, and sooner or later these same folks find themselves part of the same setting they complained about in the first place. Is there anything *you* can do to *change* things at home or work that can alter the environment? I have found for some, things weren't quite as bad as they thought they were. Another question: Are you willing to *compromise* in your current situation that troubles you, or can you *put up with* how things are? If you are willing to change something in order to make things better, then do it, but do so on a continual basis—whether it's your attitude, staying away from others who pull you down—whatever the case, *do* something. If you can put up with the situation, I recommend making the most of it. Family members don't always get along; even with the best of jobs one or two folks can bring down morale and productivity. With everything, some days, some situations are better than others.

But if you are adamant that, after everything, you cannot survive your current environment, then the only thing I can recommend is for you to get out. If you have tried everything you can and after exhausting all options, and if you wish for something better, then you have to be willing to change your environment. Again, so many folks complain how bad things are for them, but few are willing to *follow through* and do something about it. If your job is too stressful and you cannot be with your family as much as you want, then you may have to change jobs, work part-time, or find an alternate source of income. Now, the trade-off is you may not have the income you were accustomed to but are willing to give that up for better peace of mind. I have consoled countless mothers and fathers who confided in me how miserable their relationships were, even to the point of extreme domestic violence, and even though most of these individuals knew that after everything they had tried in the past their situation only became worse, they still would not leave. I would stress to them, "That's no way to live." The answer I nearly always received was something like "Well, who's gonna take care of my kids?" Or "I'll never be able to be with someone else. No one else wants me." The statements went on and on. I truly feel so bad for these folks who hate their situations, but as uncompassionate as this may sound: If *they* got themselves into their predicament, then *they*—if their environment is that bad—have to get themselves out of it.

Once again there are so many people who, when all else fails them, look for others to solve their problems. This is why I have the highest respect for single parents, like a friend of my wife's named Susan. Here's a lady who is self-employed, working seven days a week, raising her two children totally on her own, providing them a natural, caring, loving, and safe environment. When asked, "You refuse child support from your ex?" Susan smiles and says, "Yes. I broke away on my terms and didn't want anything to tie me down. It was hard. But in the end that atmosphere was killing me and my girls. I had to make a clean break. We all love each other very much and have a very happy home."

The Choice Is Yours

For many of us bad relationships, situations, or environments are extremely hard to walk away from. All of us for the most part know what we need to do, but *doing* it is something of its own. In the end for Susan, like countless others from a bad situation, it's that inner peace that truly matters.

Again, that is one of the reasons I respect those dedicated single parents so much. For the most part they work their tails off, sometimes in menial jobs, come home to a Spartan setting, and do whatever they have to in order to provide for their children and lastly themselves. In life, mistakes are made, and even with the best of intentions things don't always work out. Most of the single parents I've had the privilege of meeting, have had the courage to make the most of the situation and quite frankly don't waste their time on what could have been or how life isn't fair. Unlike the Mr. Smiths of the world, they do not blame their problems on their environment. Many single parents, no matter how despairing or ugly their environment may have been, are committed—by every ounce of themselves—to making things better for their future. They carry on. They deal with the situation, make the most of their past, and strive to carry little or no animosity from the garbage in their lives.

As always, the choice is yours.

HELP YOURSELF REMINDERS

* DON'T USE YOUR ENVIRONMENT AS A CRUTCH. IF YOU DO, YOU'LL ONLY LIMIT YOURSELF.

* IF YOU FEEL GUILTY ABOUT WHAT HAS TRANSPIRED, MAKE AMENDS AS BEST AS YOU CAN, AND IF POSSIBLE TURN IT AROUND AND USE IT AS A STEPPING-STONE TO MAKE THINGS BETTER.

* DON'T GIVE YOURSELF AWAY IN THE VAIN HOPE OF APPEASING OTHERS.

Help Yourself

* Make and maintain the commitment of being your own person.
* Limit your exposure to negative circumstances and, if possible, make the best of it.
* Above all, it's your life and your choice.

3

Learning to Forgive

It took all the reserve and discipline I had to stop myself from killing her. On a warm day during the summer of 1987, I sat in front of Mother, as an adult, while she explained in ice-cold deliberate detail the time she had stabbed me as a child. It was simply an accident, she calmly stated—as if she had spilled some milk at the breakfast table. One of "those things." When I failed to anoint her with instant forgiveness, *she* became upset, giving me a look of displeasure. She went on to justify her treatment against me further by stating, "Well, David, 'the Boy' was always in trouble. 'The Boy' deserved to be punished. 'It' was always stealing food, David. I would have fed 'It' if 'It' wasn't stealing so much. . . ." The more Mother sneered while playing another one of her sick games, the more I began to slowly feel myself consumed with an overwhelming sensation of absolute rage. As she continued her diatribe, my blood raced and I began to imagine myself throwing away my "goody-goody," "that-a-boy" lifestyle of helping others, and for once making someone pay for all the years of torture, mind games, and loneliness; transferring everything onto . . . Mother—the source of all my hatred.

I could now crystallize in my mind's eye my exact plan of kidnapping "her," stripping "her" of every normal sense of existence . . . as she had me. But now I would do it with even more relish. Since I had lived in a garage and had slept on an army cot with no blanket, I'd have her subsist in a run-down motel out in the middle of nowhere, with no heat, clothing, food, or even electricity. She would survive in total darkness. She would be without any form of human contact, just as I had been as a child when Mother had forbidden me to have any contact with my brothers. As she had used food as a weapon against me, I would only offer her bread and water, which I might or might not give her depending upon *my* mood. And not one hour of any day would pass that she would not think of me. I wouldn't kill her, but rather I'd let her mind kill her for me. I wouldn't want her to die instantly—not after all the those years when, as a child, I had existed solely as the object of her sick pleasure—no, I imagined to myself. I wanted her to feel the magnitude of what she had done to me.

Then afterward looking at Mother as she rambled on, full force, about how I had been such a burden to her and how I'd had to be put in my place, it struck me that I could simply . . . tell the authorities that . . . I had freaked out . . . from some sort of childhood posttraumatic stress. If that line worked for all the other scumbags of the universe, why shouldn't I be entitled to it? My body, which had turned ice cold before I had entered Mother's house, now seemed warm. *I could do it,* I stated to myself. *I'd have my revenge! I could become—become like* her*!*

The Need to Listen Better

All of us have said and have had wrongful thoughts during the heat of the moment. We've lashed out at our parents, our loved ones, and those at work. And I'm sure most of us regret what we may have said and the pain our actions and words may have caused. With the exception of those who are truly mentally ill, I don't believe any of us want to hurt others or carry feelings of animosity, but for some of us, particularly those who have experienced difficulty, especially if we feel we have been wronged, these feelings of bitterness may be hard to reconcile with. The truth of the matter is, those who do not deal with these feelings are almost destined to become what they detest.

For some of us these feelings of hostility may begin with something as simple as a disagreement or misunderstanding. Years ago in college the professor of my communication course taught something that sticks with me to this day—the four basic elements of communication: 1) the Messenger, 2) the Message, 3) the Receiver, and 4) the Feedback. Within these four distinctive elements is the opportunity to become confused or frustrated, especially if you put into the equation of communication that seventy percent of all communication is nonverbal, primarily referring to body language, and that twenty-three percent of all communication is pitch, tone, and the rate of the message's delivery; which only leaves about seven percent of what is actually being said. Seven percent! The biggest problem facing us as individuals, whether dealing with the opposite sex, one on one, with groups, organizations, or other nations or cultures, is *miscommunication*! Think about it: How many times have you been with a loved one, or with a coworker, or on a date, and everything seemed fine, right up until the moment you may have said or communicated the wrong message at the wrong time? You're not the only one! To this day I cannot tell you how many millions of times I have done just that. (Just ask my family.) Then, you desperately try to undo what you have already done, only to bury yourself further. Because of the miscommunication, now add the frustration we may be feeling until we're not sure what to say or do next. We doubt ourselves. Or we may not trust the actual message we are in receipt of—the messenger or the feedback we had anticipated. The biggest single component in miscommunication is we simply do not listen! Whether it's the messenger, the message, or the feedback, we do not consider what is being stressed to us. This statement rings particularly true for those we are the closest to. At times we brush off those we know and who understand us the most for reasons of complacency. At times we will take in information provided by others whom we do not know as well, even though both elements of the information are the same. We simply choose not to listen.

As the world around us continues to accelerate and as America has become more ensconced as the information capital of the world, it's easy to misinterpret the exact context of everything being thrown our way.

Lowering Your Defenses

When it comes to miscommunication, I have found that for some people the frustration stems from something simple—someone may have looked at us the wrong way or said the wrong thing to us. Again, the key words are *may have*. (Keep in mind those four elements and how we neglect to listen.) Over time this unresolved apprehension builds. I have personally been in situations in which I have met individuals who are highly agitated, yet they do not remember the reason why. All that these people know is they are upset; and for them that's all that matters. Once I joked with a person who was upset with someone by asking that person, "How long have you been mad at so-and-so?" "I've been pissed at so-and-so for over thirty-five years!" came the reply. "Well," I said, nodding my head, "that's amazing. So-and-so is only twenty-eight!" "Don't matter!" my companion countered. "That's how mad I am!"

We've all done it. All of us have judged others in the blink of an eye and processed that information before storing it into our "CD-ROM" for future reference. Then, every time we see that person or think of that particular element, like eating that one vegetable we've hated ever since we were a kid, we reopen that file that's been stored away in our brain, basing our attitude on our former judgment. (Remember the old saying about how others judge us based upon the first impression?) In other words, we have a tendency to misjudge. Have you ever met someone, then a split second later you knew you didn't like that person *until* you processed the information being presented to you differently, *then* you lowered your defenses by either relaxing or dropping your guard? Over time, if you do not change your attitude, if you keep your defenses up at maximum guard, you may find yourself continually becoming upset for really no justifiable reason—all from a simple misunderstanding.

Another example is: Have you been so upset that the words seemed to fly out of your mouth? Words you didn't truly mean? And as they spilled out, you wished you could have swallowed those words? But for some reason you kept your guard up; for above all you did not want to appear weak. Part of you knows that if you had apologized or explained yourself better, the matter could have been resolved, but seconds pass, then minutes, until a disagreement or misunderstanding goes unresolved and turns into revenge or defensiveness.

Most of us, myself included, always seem to hurt the ones we love, or the ones close to us—our significant others, our children, parents, family members, those at work, or our best friends. A psychologist I know once told me, "We take out our aggressions on those we know because we believe we can." Has this ever happened to you? I'm in a heated disagreement with my wife—the one person I am closest to, the one person on this planet whom I adore, who knows every aspect of my complex nature, my lover, my best friend, the only person I trust with all my heart—but in a disagreement I want nothing more than to prove *how wrong she is*! We banter back and forth, not listening to what either of us is trying to convey, but rather focus our efforts on wanting the other to hear our opinion. Time passes, frustration builds, hurtful things are said, and the issue goes unresolved. Neither one of us lowers our guard. I persist, determined to show my wife, my lover, my best friend, the only person I trust, the one person I wish to spend the rest of my life with, how tough I am, how hurt I have become. "Hell," I say to myself, "I'm so mad at her, I'm—I'm not gonna breathe for a week. I'm—I'm not gonna talk to her for the rest of the day . . . and night! I'm never going to talk to that woman again! Yeah, I might lose a good night's sleep, but every time I see her, I'll fire off some wisecracks just so she knows how much she's hurt me. I'm going to show her!"

Now, apply that same example toward your children—the ones who made your eyes light up when they took their first steps or made you feel such pride when you saw them in the school play. Think about your parents or guardians, those adult figures whom you felt inspired by, or that one mentor you ran to when you felt the world was going to end. Do you remember that single defining moment when that person in front of you became your best friend, your lifelong soulmate whom you shared everything with and had the best of times with by simply being together? But now you feel, for whatever reason, those people who had such a profound effect on your life, you are no longer as close as you once were. Maybe you grew in different directions, maybe you saw things differently, maybe that one disagreement became the straw that broke the camel's back, and now, with time, pride, ego, shame, resentment, or defensiveness, it keeps you from resolving the matter.

In the example of my wife and me, because we did not listen, coupled with our charged emotions, we allowed our disagreement to get the better of us. Eventually we both felt embittered and hurt. Finally, with cooler heads, when my wife and I both sat down, when we *listened*, we discovered that the issue that had made us both upset was not as bad as it had seemed during the heat of our disagreement. After making up we both forgot what it was exactly that had upset us in the first place. The element that matters is both Marsha and I do our best to resolve our issues as soon as possible, before time or an embroiled attitude can amplify the situation. Working together as a couple, like my son and me, like countless others, we try our best not to allow the sun to set without trying to find some form of resolution to whatever may be troubling us. I may not solve all the problems with my son who, let's say, is adamant about dying his hair orange, but I will still hug him good-night and tell him how much I love him. My reference is almost like the one

I read some time ago that stated: A couple should never bring their argument into the sanctuary of their bedroom. As stressed in Chapter One, if we have an unresolved issue, over time those feelings may not only consume us but may even give rise to further problems.

Even with the "best of friends," the "perfect parents," the "perfect marriage," the "greatest job," or the "greatest clients" in the world, if there were two people stranded on a deserted island they would eventually get on each others' nerves. As long as there is more than one person in the world, there will always be trouble in paradise. I am only trying to stress the importance of solving an issue before it comes to a head; before it leads to anger, outrage, or brews into feelings of hatred.

Not to get on my soapbox, but I cannot begin to tell you how many people I have met, how many folks I have known over the course of my life, who have wasted, and I do mean *wasted*, a large part of their time, energy, and life force proving to *that* person, *that* parent, *that* boss, or *whoever* else, how wrong *they* were. Can you imagine being on your deathbed when you finally forgave *that* person or brought closure to *that* issue that had dominated your life for so long? With all due respect to you: that in itself would be a tragedy.

In May of 1991, while in Salt Lake City visiting a relative, out of the blue I received a distressing phone call from Mother. The next day I rushed over and saw a person I could barely recognize. Slumped in the same worn-out recliner chair in which I'd seen her in the summer of

1987 was the person who had tried to take out her revenge on me, but had now become a victim of her own hate. Her halfhearted smile only exposed Mother's darkened yellow teeth. Her face was puffy and dark red and her once shiny, perfume-scented hair was now greasy and matted against the sides of her face. Mother claimed she would cry out in pain whenever she tried to walk because her feet were so swollen. Unless Mother clasped her hands, they would constantly shake.

Mother's hygiene reflected the appearance of her home. After surveying her unkept living room, I sensed Mother knew she didn't have much time left. After a few hollow pleasantries, with glee Mother quickly launched into her never-ending rants about how her mother had done this to her, that to her, how hard, cruel, and unfair life was for Mother. Building on her own tempo, Mother went on to boast, "I'll tell you what! I showed your grandmother. I showed her! She can't control me! No one, no one's gonna tell me what to do. Not now, not ever!"

Whatever feelings of shame or anger that had bubbled to the surface before I came face to face with Mother once again, slowly washed away. All I could do was nod my head at the end of Mother's diatribes. I was in no way agreeing with what she said, but rather educating myself that this was a complete waste of Mother's time, energy, and life. A majority of her life, from what I had seen for over twenty-five years, was built on revenge and hate. Finally, after expelling her frustrations, for a rare fleeting moment Mother dropped her defenses and I was able to see through her facade and how absolutely broken and completely lonely Mother had become. All I could say to myself was *what a waste*. More than ever, I renewed my vow to not travel down the same path as Mother had.

Never Go to Bed Upset

This is why when I work with teenagers, whom I address as "young adults," I often joke with them, stressing, "Never never go to bed upset! If you're that annoyed with your parents, if you feel the need, burst through their bedroom door, march up to them, and state, 'Mother, Father, I know you may be concerned about my spiky green hairdo, outrageous loud music, and my neurotic friends. But it's gonna be okay. I love you. I know right from wrong; I just want to be my own person. Not to worry, it's gonna be fine!' " If you're a teenager and you act like a child, you will be treated as a child. If, however, you wish to be treated as a young adult, take some accountability, and understand that in life when dealing with others—no matter who it is you're dealing with or how old you are—it's a matter of give and take: in order to have "this" you have to be willing to give up "that." So, when talking to your parents or guardians, don't beat around the bush, but get right to it; whether it's about dating, insecurity, sex, peer pressure, school, whatever. Lower your defenses and open up your heart. Even if you or your parents say something in the heat of the moment, I implore you not to develop the *attitude* and shut them out. Don't use your frustration as a way of getting back at them—*I'm gonna show them a thing or two; I'm gonna date him/her 'cause I know it's going to drive my parents crazy! I'm gonna do whatever I please, whenever I please!* If you begin to act in such a way, it may become a habit, which can become a lifestyle of self-destruction, and don't you deserve better than that? And, *who* are you really hurting? All I'm trying to say is as a young adult, before you develop *that* kind of attitude, think long and hard about the consequences of your decisions and where they can lead you to in the future.

Think of my mother! Here's a person who somehow got caught up in her own unresolved issues, developed that I'm-gonna-show-her! attitude that led to a destructive rampage, until she wasted her life by all the hell she put everyone and herself through right up until the moment she finally died.

After assisting others for over sixteen years, I have found that most parents/guardians are just plain scared when it comes to raising you. They simply don't want you to repeat the same mistakes they have made and desire for you to have the opportunity to live a better life. That's it! They want you to succeed! Some are even scared to death with all the temptation "out there." Those who've raised you are terrified of something bad happening to you. Think about it from their position: You are in the most important stage of your life, transitioning into adulthood or what others call "breaking away." For a lot of parents and guardians it's an impossible balancing act of trying to protect you from the atrocities of the world, while trying to prepare you for what's on the outside as well. My advice: Use your head, keep your cool, give them respect, and act accordingly. You *will* make a lot of mistakes (that's how you learn in life), and your parents or guardians know this. But don't lose yourself in the process. At the end of the day, when you go to bed upset or feeling vengeful, ask yourself this: *Who am I really hurting?*

Parents/guardians, if you find you are having a hard time getting through to your teenager, even when things seem grim keep the channels of communication open. Break down any barrier you can. Maintain your standard while relating with these young adults *at their level.* I have found that, as much as teens crave independence, they still desire nurturing guidance. Even when things seem volatile, as best as you can lower your defenses and speak from your heart. If possible, relate to them on a personal, not parental, level. Reveal your feelings of anxiety, elements of *your past,* and anything that can help alleviate any tension. Such as the type of clothes you wore at their age, the kind of music your parents thought was either smutty, ear shattering, or "satanic," or how strange your friends were at the time. As upset as they may be, and as much as you may disagree with your teenager, explain to them the importance of their choices, where their decisions can lead them, and most importantly end your discussion on a positive note.

You can use the same approach when dealing with those at work. I know of so many who dedicate their time and energy on either getting even or the I'll-show-them! attitude, to the point of sabotaging the business and themselves in the process. So, when a disagreement or problem arises, rather than brushing it aside and hoping for the best, take a stand and set a standard as a leader by addressing the situation as expeditiously as possible. Investigate all options that may be available to find a solution to the dilemma while trying to maintain the morale of those around you. I believe team members do not mind a serious critique, so long as they are treated with respect. A great deal of productivity can be saved when issues are solved before feelings of animosity take root.

Compromise

Rather than hold a grudge and waste your time hashing over who did what to whom, get to the core of the frustration. If necessary, be the bigger person—compromise and give a little. Don't shut that person down. Don't let powerful, negative emotions get the best of you. Open your heart and make an effort to resolve the situation as best as you can. Even if the issue is not totally resolved, at least you'll have less gnawing at you, you'll feel a little bit cleansed by trying to work through it, *and* you will be less likely to harbor ill feelings. Again, life is not perfect. Not all situations are black and white, to be solved like they are at the end of a sitcom television show. Next time when you find yourself in the middle of a disagreement, instead of proving yourself give a little. When dealing with those close to me, I have learned that sometimes the smallest things—a touch, hug, or a kind word—can make a world of difference. Resolve the matter before it envelopes you. Before your feelings become ensconced . . . and perhaps lead to hate.

The Cancer of Hate

Of all the lessons I have been fortunate enough to learn, the single most powerful, most important one is: Hate no one! If you get nothing else from this book, please, I beg of you, take this advice with you. As a child, I saw firsthand *how much* my mother hated everyone and everything. I can only assume her hatred began with some unresolved issue from her past. She then turned her anger against her mother, her husband, my brothers, her brother and his family, her dearest and closest friends, and, for whatever reason, her hatred nearly killed me, her own son. As a young boy I saw how quickly Mother's feelings of animosity went from one person to another, then another, until it spread to everything connected in her life.

I believe hate is like cancer: it can spread and kill a person, one "life cell," one day, at a time. If hatred goes unchecked it can take over one's life, as it did to my mother and others like her. If you hate today, it's easier for you to hate tomorrow, then the next day and the next, until you've wasted your entire life by becoming dominated by what you detested in the first place. The only cure for the cancer of hatred is dealing with the problem as best as you can, while releasing any animosity you may have. My question to you is: How can you live a productive life and all that goes with it, if you are controlled by intense feelings such as hate? Personally, I don't call that much of a life.

I recently read an article in a national magazine that addressed the issue of letting go of hate. The article made reference to Mitchell Wright, the widower of Shannon Wright, a teacher who was killed at the school shooting in Jonesboro, Arkansas. Before Shannon died she said to Mitchell, "Take care of Zane," their baby boy. While there may be some who would probably say Mitchell has every reason to hate those who have caused such great pain and loss in his life and his son's life, it is Mitchell who said, "If you let the hate and anger build in you, that's a very strong sin. I need to be able to totally forgive. Well, if I lose it, then I can't take care of Zane."

The same article also discussed a study at the Templeton Foundation Campaign for Forgiveness Research where psychotherapists stated that the psychological effects of forgiveness help dissipate anger, improve personal relationships, and help banish depression. The feature then quoted Charlotte Witvliet, a professor in psychology at Hope College, who suggests, through her extensive studies, that we may hold grudges ". . . because that makes us feel like we are more in control and we are less sad." Like others in her field who believe in empathy, Ms. Witvliet continues, "If you are willing to exert the effort it takes to be forgiving, there are benefits both emotionally and physically."

With all the animosity that seems to resonate within our society, I cannot overemphasize the power of forgiveness. In all the years I have assisted others, I have *never* met anyone who woke up with the sole intention of overdosing on drugs or alcohol, killing themselves, or hurting others. Something led them to it. While there are some who adamantly made excuses, I've found that most of these people believe that a series of events, coupled with deep frustration, led them to their course of action. Unresolved issues, bad situations, and feelings of animosity over time became a habitual lifestyle. These individuals, like my mother, became consumed with their own hate.

I think of my mother's life as a tragedy. Before things became very bad between us, I remember her as a beautiful, caring woman who wanted nothing more than to live for her children. As a child I used to pray for my *mommy* to wake up from her drunken state and take me in her arms so we could live happily ever after. Yet, as the years passed, I knew something had a hold over my mother's goodness. She pushed down whatever feelings troubled her, became addicted to alcohol, and ultimately treated me as she did. A lot of people are quick to state that it was because she was simply an alcoholic. I think Mother drank, like others who abuse drugs or alcohol, largely to mask whatever was gnawing at her.

At the time when Mother was raised, America was far more restricted than it is today, especially for women.

During my mother's time there was little help or professional guidance available for her.

I am not making excuses or defending my mother's actions, but what can you take with you, what can you learn from my mother's calamity and others like her? Right now, YOU have a choice. In this informational age that we live in there are infinite resources to help you work through practically any issues that seem to be pulling you down. And because our society is becoming more open, we can talk about things—AIDS, cancer, child abuse, spousal abuse, sexual preferences, just to name a few—that we would not only never have uttered in public, but deliberately kept in the closet just a short time ago. As an individual you have the power to choose. You can either work through your anxieties or become a slave to them, like my mother. Like a lot of things in life, dealing with frustration or feelings of animosity is not going to be easy. But you deserve a life of happiness and the opportunity to do whatever you want, rather than dread and sorrow that you will have to live with the rest of your days.

When I worked in juvenile hall, I would see teenagers who would often hurt others in the exact manner in which they had been harmed, but with far more cruelty and relish. When I asked them why, the reply I usually received was "I want them to feel what I felt and then some, so I won't be hurt again!" *When does it end?* How much does it take? How tough do we have to act, how much pain do we have to inflict on others, how much of ourselves do we have to lose in order to prove ourselves to others? After mankind has been on this planet for thousands of years, fighting endless wars, and with the millions upon millions who have died, the world is not enough. For some, all the hatred they keep locked away in their hearts will never satisfy whatever ails them. As tough as they may act, as much pain as they may inflict on themselves and others, as much as they may lose themselves in denial, drugs, booze, or instant-gratification relationships, the frustration and anger will always dominate their lives. I believe *you* deserve better than that!

Do not become trapped by your hatred. My mother died a very lonely person. When I was very young, I thought Mother was the epitome of regal—the way she smiled when she strolled into a room, the sound of her soothing voice—she was my princess mommy. The most outgoing, caring person with a perfect house, prized flower garden, and model family. Yet, her anger toward herself, then directed toward others, made her into an unkempt, overweight alcoholic, living in a house that I can only describe as vile. Alone, the only contact she had with the outside world was basically whatever she saw on television. As lonely as Mother became, she would, at least when I saw her, instantly recite how she had been wronged in her life. Her body would shake and her face would turn crimson as she would recite how much she detested everyone and everything in her life. Think of it: a lifetime wasted. Minute after minute, day after day, year after year . . . wasted. A person with unresolved issues, who became trapped by her own hate.

Forgiveness

I am always asked if I hate my mother. Without hesitation I respond with a resounding *no*! I saw firsthand, through the eyes of a bewildered child, the changes within Mother and the damage they inflicted on my brothers, my father, others, and me. As a child, the time I spent sitting on top of my hands at the base of the staircase in the dark garage gave me time to think. During one of those lonely hours, I came to realize that if Mother's hate had made her as she was, then I would be different. . . . *I had to be different.* At times when she would beat me to the point I could not even crawl away, I vowed to be nothing like her. While in foster care, some of my teenage friends would either cop out or quit on themselves at any kind of minor obstacle that was in their path or immediately flare up and act tough. Some of them tried to drown the pain and animosity by picking on others, or with drugs and alcohol. Eventually some of them became slaves to their outlets and found themselves being controlled all over again.

Even now, as an adult, I come in contact with so many people who are still tied to their past partly because of their unpleasant emotions. I have a dear friend, Barbara, who years ago was happily married. But after ten years the union ended in divorce. That was nearly twenty years ago, and whenever I spoke to her, after we would exchange initial salutations, I could sense her breathing accelerating and the slight change in her voice as she exploded into the phone, ranting about how her ex-husband had done this or did that, until she became so worked up that I feared she might have passed out from hyperventilation. Barbara would become so upset and lost in her berating that she'd forget she'd been complaining to me about the exact same things for almost two decades! She would "loop"; her mind would just run in circles. For Barbara it seemed to never end. Over the years Barbara had spent more time and energy putting down her former husband than she had spent being married to him.

Once, after Barbara calmed down, I gently reminded her that, as a couple, they had spent *some* good times together, at least enough to have stayed married for ten years and had two beautiful children whom they both adore. Yet I think Barbara, without knowing, as most of us do when intimate feelings are involved, got caught up in taking a stroll down vengeance lane for so long that it became a habitual response whenever she thought of her former husband. Unlike my mother, Barbara is a caring, functional, responsible person who, once she became aware of her vindictive emotional state, began to forgive her former husband and move on with her life.

When I stress *forgiveness,* I do so mainly to encourage freeing yourself. To me, forgiveness does not mean forgetting what may have happened to or against you. And, like grieving, forgiveness takes time just like any emotion. Forgiveness doesn't happen overnight. But with time, maturity, and a different perspective we can free ourselves of emotions that can only lead to great suffering.

Noted psychologist Bernie Zilbergeld echoes my thoughts. Mr. Zilbergeld states: "Holding a grudge is one of the most self-destructive things you can do. If you want to have a happy life, you have to move on and let go."

Today my mother, I believe with all my heart, is in heaven and finally resting in peace. Not a day passes that I do not think of her. I believe she was a person who carried so much pain within the deepest recesses of her heart. Maybe I had to learn from Mother's unfortunate lifestyle how *not* to live my life.

In forgiving my perpetrator, I feel cleaner. It frees me to not only live a more fulfilled life, but, more importantly, to rid myself of any animosity. I am able to love my wife, my son, and life all the more. When we elect to hate, we not only lose our compassion for others but we lose ourselves in the process. Keep in mind that for someone to hurt you, someone must have hurt them too.

Hate no one. Get closure with the person you need to forgive. Pick up that phone, talk to that person, write that letter even if you never mail it. Hug that person. Lower your defenses. Listen with your heart and an objective mind. Just do whatever you have to do to expel those bad feelings from your system. Every day, wipe your slate clean.

* * *

To me, getting rid of the garbage in our lives is like taking out the daily trash. Every day we toss out rotten food, used newspapers, and, for some, those soiled diapers we don't want to touch with a ten-foot pole. But, once we do, we wash our hands and never give it a second thought. Yet, somehow we allow the psychological garbage from our lives to rot away our esteem . . . day after day after day. To keep ourselves from deteriorating, we need to look at our situations for what they were, take some form of action now, and let the past go.

If you harbor ill feelings, if you stay in a negative environment and do not deal with troubling situations, you can only go so far in life. You may have the world in the palm of your hand, but at the cost of running away from yourself. Every day when you get up and look at yourself in the mirror, you will see yourself as who you truly are and the baggage and disparity you carry—*every day* for the rest of your life. You will be so busy with all the troubles of your world, you will lose sight of what truly matters in your life. Again, I ask you: With all that you have experienced and as unhappy as you may be, don't you deserve better than that? *I believe you do!*

HELP YOURSELF REMINDERS

* LISTEN NOT ONLY TO WHAT IS BEING SAID, BUT TO THE MESSAGE BEHIND THE WORDS.

* LOWER YOUR GUARD.

* CONSTANTLY DO YOUR BEST TO RESOLVE WHATEVER PROBLEMS YOU HAVE.
* COMPROMISE, AT LEAST JUST ENOUGH TO MAKE THINGS BETTER.
* HATE, JUST LIKE CANCER, IF NOT DEALT WITH EARLY ON, KILLS ONE DAY AT A TIME.
* FORGIVENESS ALLOWS YOU TO BE CLEANSED AND HELPS TO EASE YOUR PAIN.

Part Two

Know What You Want out of Your Life

4

The One Thing

Over and over I had kept thinking, *This is it*. My knees were shaking, not because I was eight years old and had been embarrassed standing in front of Mother wearing only my underwear briefs, but because by the look in her eyes I truly believed Mother was going to kill me. Of all the "games" Mother played against me, she had never acted as she did that day when my father was away at work and my two brothers, Ron and Stan, were at their Boy Scout meeting. That afternoon as Mother screeched, my mind raced to find a way out. "Today," Mother had bellowed, "I saw—I saw 'the Boy' playing on the school grass!"

As I had for years, I simply stood in front of Mother dumbfounded. Since the age of four I had done my best to keep our secret between Mother and me. But by the time I was eight, I had felt the games were getting out of control. One day Mother had taken a drastic turn exposing our secret further by announcing to my brothers that

I was no longer a member of the family; that I was to be addressed as "the Boy." She then threatened my two brothers Ron and Stan; they were not allowed to talk to or even look at the Boy, otherwise they'd receive the same treatment as I did. As always I remained docile, retreating further inside my shell. Back then, no matter what Mother did to me, I kept my mouth shut. I buried my feelings of fear, frustration, and the sense of shame deep inside. From the bottom of my heart I truly believed everything was my fault—if Mother had a bad hair day; if she stubbed her toe; somehow, some way, it was my fault and there would be hell to pay. I had replayed in my mind the countless times I was punished and knew it had to be me because I never did anything to stop her. Part of me so desperately wanted to believe things weren't as bad as they were between Mother and me. I remembered how years ago Mommy, after kissing Ron and Stan good-night, would sometimes bend down whispering how sorry she was, that things had simply just got out of hand, or that she had had a bad day. As always I prayed, aching with all of my heart, that things between Mother and me would get better.

Yet that afternoon, although my knees were shaking, I remained motionless. My mind tried to understand Mother's statement of "the Boy playing on the school grass." But it did not make any sense to me. For years I had allowed Mother to control me—to the point that I never did anything without first asking for her approval. I knew the Boy was absolutely forbidden to play, stand on, or even touch the school grass. *"But how?"* I had thought to myself. *"How could this be?"* Finding no answer, I believed it was simply a mix-up. At times Mother had claimed she would drive to the school during lunch to watch her *two* children play. That day, I had figured, Mother must have mistaken me for another kid.

My analysis was interrupted as Mother again thundered how I not only had played on the school grass, but how she caught me rolling around, flailing like a madman. The more Mother ranted, the better I felt. I knew it was a mistake. A simple mistake. Mother's claims were completely unfounded, and I thought to myself that as soon as I tell Mother the truth, as soon as she looks down at my unmarked, pressed pants, she'll let it go. Just as soon as I tell her.

But my dilemma was that I was not allowed to speak unless granted permission to do so. I was not even allowed to gaze at Mother's face without her approval. Even though I had known this entire matter could have been resolved within the blink of an eye, I deliberately did not do a thing. I did not move my finger to point to my unstained pants; I did not utter a syllable; but I did lift my head to have Mother search within my heart. I had been more terrified of what she would do to me if I violated her rules than of whatever she had in store for me. Even though I had felt trapped between two separate worlds, I remained docile and once again provided Mother with another opportunity to punish me for a crime I had not committed.

That day at that moment, when I refused to do anything, I despised myself. I never did anything to stop

Mother. I never uttered a response to her accusation, I never defended myself, and I never walked out the door. I never stood up for myself and stopped Mother dead in her tracks with a single word: I never said no. So I thought that maybe I somehow deserved or even wanted to be treated as I had been. Either way, I had known Mother was out of control, and my only response had been to stand in front of her, with my head bent down, eyes fixed on the multicolored spotted kitchen floor, with my mouth tightly shut, waiting to endure the brunt of Mother's madness.

"Look at me!" Mother exploded, with a finger thrust toward my face. "For years you, you've made my life a living hell! You're the reason your father and I argue, you're the reason why I drink, why I feel so bad! You've made my life a living hell, so now I'm going to show you what hell is all about!" With that Mother stepped over and flipped on the burners to the gas stove. Even as my mind screamed for me to flee, yell at the top of my lungs, wish myself to become invisible, to do something, anything, I remained immobile. In a flash Mother seized the tips of my fingers of my right hand, dragging me over to the stove before holding my exposed forearm to the flames. As I yelled, emptying my lungs, I could not believe what was happening to me.

The instant Mother released her grip, I fell to the floor licking my arm. Through my tears I saw her standing above me with her hands on her hips, when she announced, "Now, I want the Boy to lay down on the stove and burn for me!" Part of me became numb. I had somehow thought that Mother would bend down and scoop me into her arms before racing me off to the hospital. Yet at the time, over and over my mind repeated, *I still can't believe it! This can't be happening!*

At the snap of Mother's fingers, while cradling my arm I stood with my head bent down, exactly three feet in front of her in my "position of address." Even though my arm began to throb, I gave it little attention. I blocked out the pain thinking of what I could do next. With tears in my eyes, I took a chance and stole a glance at Mother, in the veiled hope that she would see I had somehow learned my lesson, that I would never do again whatever she claimed I had done. Surely, I believed, Mother had taken her game as far as she dared.

"I said," Mother bellowed, "I want you to lay down on this stove and burn for me." With no more tears to cry, and my muscles feeling like Jell-O, I stared at the stove until I imagined myself on top of it. I gave up. I knew there was nothing I could do. Mother was always right: I was the Boy who deserved to be punished.

Without thinking, I looked up at Mother. While clutching a glass in her hand, she cocked her head to one side smiling. *She really wants me to do it,* I told myself, *She really wants me to lay down on the stove and burn, burn for her!* This wasn't another game, I thought. She knew: if I obeyed her command, I was going to die.

At that moment I became so scared, so terrified of dying, I had to do something, anything, to stop Mother. At that precise time in my life, nothing else mattered. Yet, I didn't budge. I didn't flee or scream out how sick she was. For some reason I had transfixed my attention on the kitchen clock that was stained with grease and dust and hung just above the doorway beside a set of copper-colored baking molds.

Everything seemed to slow down. As I focused my attention at the red second hand that swept past the black numbers of the clock, my fear and even my throbbing arm seemed almost distant. It was then I had noticed that the two other hands to the clock read ten minutes to four. *Ten minutes to four!* Suddenly it hit me: my brothers Ron and Stan . . . they would be home from Boy Scouts at four o'clock. . . . So, if I could slow her down . . . if *I* could steal ten minutes' worth of time, *maybe today I won't die!*

The answer was that simple. I would do whatever I had to in order to stay away from the gas stove. Mother could beat me, spit at me, berate me, or break every bone in my body; just as long as she didn't kill me, I did not care. Since Mother's games had been a closely guarded secret for years, she would never think of acting as she just had in front of Ron and Stan—who were closer to exposing Mother's latest game and saving me with every passing second. By focusing my entire being on stealing ten minutes' worth of time, I did so one second at a time. I had stepped out of my obedient servant mode and, without knowing, applied a form of passive resistance.

As Mother continued to screech at me, without permission I slowly ran my eyes up her body until I met hers. Without permission I spoke. By automatic reflex Mother raised her hand. I then lay crumpled on the kitchen floor. While Mother bellowed on and on, between taking gulps from her glass, I counted: *Forty-eight, forty-seven, forty-six. . . .* Then, with a snap of Mother's fingers I was required to stand in front of her within one second. *I took three.* Since before kindergarten, I had been conditioned to stand in the position of address: exactly three feet in front of Mother, within striking distance. That afternoon when I stood in front of her, I deliberately took a half step backward, extending my distance a few extra inches. I did so knowing full well when Mother would hit me, *she* would have to adjust and take a step closer to strike me; thus, wasting more time.

My strategy worked. Mother had no idea *I was working her*. The pattern repeated itself every few seconds until I extended my ploy further by stuttering. Amazingly Mother tilted her head, waiting for me to complete my sentence before berating me, then hitting me until I landed on the floor. Mother again snapped her fingers, commanding me to assume the position of address. Counting backward, I took a couple of deep breaths before wobbling in front of her. While I carefully slid one foot at a time backward, until the cycle had replayed itself again, again, and again. Every time the side of my face struck the kitchen floor and tiny silver stars filled my vision, I smiled. As Mother lashed out at me, I wiped the blood from my nose and squinted at the clock's red hand making its way closer to my goal.

By sheer luck my oldest brother, Ron, came home five minutes early. Stealing another glance at Mother, I saw the blood instantly drain from her face—she had not expected Ron to come home so soon either. The second after Mother heard the front door open, she grabbed my clothes and threw them and me down the staircase to the garage. At the bottom of the stairs I dressed in the dark. I began to shiver. So many emotions began to take over. At the time I desperately wanted to convince Mother, to prove to her beyond any doubt, that I had not played on the school grass. I began yelling at myself, saying if only I were better—if only I brought home better grades; did my chores faster, better. If only I'd stop screwing up and making Mother so furious—then maybe, just maybe, I would be worthy of her love.

Without knowing, I found myself purging every emotion I had kept buried deep within my heart for the last four years. What began as a trickle became a waterfall of tears. I knew that "big boys don't cry," but I didn't care. I let everything out. The more I opened up to myself, the more I came to realize: no matter what I did—if I brought home the best grades on my report card; if I completed the dinner dishes in fifteen minutes rather than thirty; if by some chance I had one, just one day in which I was absolutely perfect for her—Mother would hate me just the same. As my mind replayed everything that had just happened, I suddenly realized *I* was not forcing Mother to drink; I was not solely responsible for the arguments between my parents. I kept thinking over and over again, *I* was not putting a gun to my mother's head and having her pull the trigger. Yes, I was slow and it took me forever to do anything; I was stupid, and somehow I had always landed myself in some sort of hot water, but *Mother*, not *I*, was responsible for her actions against me.

When I understood that I was not solely accountable for Mother's rage, I felt a trembling sensation that ran from my legs to my arms. In the blackness of the garage, where I believed giant snakes and other swamplike creatures lived that could snatch me away at any second, I looked down at my right arm, which I had forgotten about during my moments of purging, but which now seemed to throb with pain. I had focused so much energy on manipulating Mother by stealing time, that I had somehow suppressed my burn. After I had gently brushed off the tiny burnt hairs, I could see blisters beginning to form. Holding my arm and feeling the sensation of cool air when I blew on it had meant only one thing: *I was alive!* If I could feel my arm throb, then it meant I wasn't dead. If I wasn't dead, it meant that Mother hadn't killed me. I was alive! I had won! I gave it everything I had. I had come up with an instantaneous plan, focused on every move, every breath I took; paid the price to steal a few seconds of precious time, and I beat a drunken adult. I won. Lowering my arm, I shook off my fear of the imaginary serpents and stood just a little taller. I thought to myself, *If I could accomplish what I just did* against Mother and survive, *what could I not possibly do?*

While my knees had vibrated from a rush of emotions and shock beginning to take hold, I made a vow. As I had raised my arm, I could feel the blisters rub against my bicep. Not caring if anyone heard me, I stated, "No matter what happens from this moment on, I am going to give everything my best shot. No matter what happens . . . from this moment on, I will never, ever quit."

The one thing I wanted, the one thing I craved more than anything, was to remain alive.

Your Defining Moment

I realize the preceding may seem harsh or even brutal, but as terrifying as it was for me, that one incident became the turning point of my life. For the first time in my life, I found myself in what I believed was a deadly situation that forced me not only to concentrate on what truly mattered but to take some form of action for myself. Above all, because of that one situation I was fortunate enough to take something with me that I'm still able to apply each and every day.

And again, my example is not a gruesome illustration for the purpose of exploitation or to extract sympathy. Think of it this way: If that *child*—whether it was me or anyone else, for that matter—could endure, alter, and survive that situation without any help, without any professional training, coaching, or college degree, let alone a great deal of practical experience, what is stopping *you* from achieving your desires?

My intention is to help you realize the indomitable human spirit within us all. Many predicaments in our lives are unexpected and we may not be up to the initial challenge. It may even seem overwhelming. But, as explained in the first section of this book, as individuals we can either run from our situations, bury them, or face our problems and deal with them accordingly.

When negative situations arise, it is mainly up to you as an individual to address them and take some form of action in order to deal with them. It comes down to choice: you can let your brain spin like that CD-ROM we posited earlier, telling yourself life isn't fair, that you're a victim, or get so scared that you become immobile; *or* you can at least try to do something, anything, about the problem at hand. At that time, I would rather have had Mother do anything she damn well pleased, just as long as she didn't burn me—I simply did what I had to do.

As naive as I was, my first form of defense was to become aware of the gravity of my situation. Being aware and fearful of any possible outcome, I had to think for myself, then take some form of action, which happened to be passive resistance. I blocked out the pain from my arm and focused on stealing whatever precious time I could. Afterward, at the bottom of the stairs, I purged my emotions, understanding for the first time the extent of my situation that for years I had denied. I felt utterly helpless, but decided I had to do something *for* myself. Coming to realize what I had just accomplished by manipulating Mother, I used that as a mental platform to build upon. Making a declaration to myself—in a child's viewpoint seeing things as black and white, right or wrong, with no room for ambiguity—from that moment on I had to think ahead and plan for any event or situation before it happened. Doing so not only relieved some of the pain and loneliness, but kept my mind sharp and on the offensive.

You Do Not Need to Be a Victim

Just because bad things happen to you, or unexpected situations arise, doesn't mean you are destined to be a victim. Years ago when I flew for the air force, before any of the crew stepped aboard the aircraft we would address various possible in-flight emergencies that might occur, then step by step go over the exact sequence we would initiate in order to counter the event. Because of the dangers inherent in flying, when something unforeseen did arise, we had thought ahead and our responses were calm and automatic; we didn't stop and whine, getting ourselves into an emotional state that would take our focus away from what needed to be accomplished. None of us was a robot or an Einstein, but simply an individual determined not to succumb to a negative situation. After every in-flight event I always walked away a better, wiser person. Ask yourself this: When you faced a situation and did your absolute best, even if it wasn't the exact outcome you desired, weren't you able to use that as a catalyst to change other parts of your life? A milestone to look back on to draw strength from? Again, if you can do that by yourself, without a great deal of help or professional guidance or training, what can you not possibly achieve?

When you know what you want and either physical or

emotional pain is involved, think of women giving birth and the hours of labor they endure. Some mothers have told me that during labor, rather than focusing on their anguish, they detach themselves and think how soon they will be able to hold their babies. In a sense the same goes for those who play sports. When a slight injury occurs, the players get right back up and focus on the task at hand. To achieve what you want, you do what you have to do!

All of us have had and will continue to face issues in our lives for the rest of our lives. Nothing and no one on this planet can stop it. It's a fact of life. Someone once said that it is not one's external but his internal environment that truly counts. So, *your* attitude is everything.

Prisoners of war, who have endured years of extreme torture and solitude, have applied the same techniques of detaching from their negative circumstances and concentrated instead on what truly mattered to them: survival with a sense of honor. Not willing to give up, many of them harnessed their internal environment, using their solitude to solve mathematical equations. I have studied one American officer who built a house in his head. This person began by formulating a blueprint in his mind. Next, he laid the foundation, built the frame, and visualized every beam, every window, and didn't stop until he had imagined himself placing every room with the exact furniture. Years later the officer stated, "I knew how grave my situation was. I alone had to do something about it. Accepting the hand I was dealt, I knew I couldn't escape and knowing the enemy's sole intention was to break us and get inside our heads, I kept my sanity by changing how and what I thought about." This same man now claims that because he had survived what he had, when he now faces a situation he taps back into what got him through before, "when it really mattered."

Whenever I'm asked, "Dave, when did your life turn around for you? When did things get better?" by habit I rub my right arm and tell the story of my being burned and what I had to do at the time. I wasn't courageous, not all that bright, but I—like countless others forced to confront a dilemma—did what I had to at the time. Taking some form of responsibility over that *one* situation allowed me to open a door and steer my mind in a completely different direction. With one sentence: *If I could survive Mother trying to kill me, what can I not possibly achieve?* my entire attitude, my entire life, changed for the better.

Creating Better Options

After making my vow, rather than feeling dejected, I was able to shed years of feeling stupid and worthless. Deep inside I knew better. It didn't happen overnight, but day by day I began to believe in myself. All I did was maintain my focus. I accepted my situation for what it was and took some form of action to make my circumstance just a little bit better. As a child alone at the bottom of the stairs, I spent countless hours imagining with perfect clarity what I would do *before* anything happened to me. For instance, when Mother would walk down the hallway, if I was in her way I was required, no matter what chore I was doing, to stop and stand erect in the position of address with my back against the wall. Before, Mother would hit me and I'd instantly collapse on the floor in pain. But since making my vow and knowing there was nothing I could do to change Mother's behavior, when the same situation occurred I was able to initiate my plan—which I had analyzed to the smallest detail. Because I was not allowed to look at Mother as she came near me and was not allowed to wear my glasses, I'd focus instead on listening to the speed of her approach. Then, before Mother would raise her hand to strike, I'd turn my head down and in the opposite direction of her. Knowing that she usually hit me on the upper part of my chest, by making a slight adjustment in my stance I'd expose and tighten that part of my chest so it didn't hurt as much as before. Later on I would even tighten the upper part of my arms, forcing my upper chest to harden all the more. This was years before I learned of the word *kinesiology*, the movement of muscles. And, this in no way prevented my mother from attacking me. My detailed plan wasn't foolproof. But at least I was a little better off than I had been before. And at the time that was enough to get me through.

Mother would refuse to feed me for whatever reason she'd choose. If I looked at her without permission, breathed in front of her, or if I did not clear the dinner table and wash, dry, and put the dishes away in ten minutes or less, my punishment was starvation. Realizing whatever I did or didn't do was futile, I resolved to come up with a plan to feed myself. I was fully aware that stealing was wrong, but at the time I believed it was my only way to survive. I began by snatching bits of food from the refrigerator. When I was caught, I later stole food from the downstairs pantry. When I was discovered there, I scrounged food from the garbage can in the garage.

When I could no longer find enough food at home, I began stealing lunches from my classmates before school would start. Thinking ahead, I'd drop to one knee so I could shield what I was doing as I rummaged through the brown paper bags and metal lunch boxes. Not wanting the other kids to go hungry, I'd snatch a sandwich wrapped in wax paper, take half of it, then replace the other half. Other times I'd grab an apple and take a few bites before putting the fruit back exactly where I'd found it. Over the course of a few weeks everyone realized someone was taking food from the lunches, so the staff kept them locked up in the classroom closets. When that option expired, my next plan was sneaking into the cafeteria, until someone found me stealing frozen hot dogs and Tater Tots.

One day during lunchtime recess, not having eaten for more than a day, I became envious of the other kids who had just had lunch, and were playing and laughing without a care in the world. I turned ice cold to everything I was seeing. I threw my hands up in disgust, yelling to myself how unfair life was. How *they* had more than me, a better life than me, and didn't have to live like I did. They had better clothes than me, nicer parents, ate food whenever they pleased, were able to sleep in a real bed. . . . The list became endless. Inside my head, I threw a temper tantrum, screaming, *"Life isn't fair! Life isn't fair!"* over and over, until I became filled with hate and jealousy.

I was completely right and completely wrong. I realize this may be hard to swallow, but the cold reality is: *Life is not now nor ever will be fair.* Period. Someone else always appears to have more, live better, or achieve whatever they want without the slightest effort. It seems that *they* will have better clothes, nicer parents, more fulfilled relationships, perfect, obedient children, superior health, nicer bodies, and surround themselves with fancier lifestyles. It seems that others who do not apply or dedicate themselves as much as you, will drive around in that new car, live in a bigger house, receive that promotion, have a corner office with windows . . . blah, blah, blah, blah. And there is little you can do about it. As I emphasized before, it's important to recognize your situation for what it is, let out feelings of frustration, deal with it, then let it go. But you need to be careful not to find yourself trapped in a vicious circle of complaining or of letting your emotions get the best of you about things you have absolutely no control over. In that sense, I was completely wrong when I yelled "Life isn't fair!" It is very disheartening to know there are scores of people who rant endlessly, jump up and down, or go down that endless hallway about something from their past, about how unfair such and such was or how they got ripped off, *rather than* taking stock in themselves, being realistic about the dilemma, and doing something positive about it for themselves!

Maybe it's a good thing that life isn't fair. When you're behind a little, that's when you're focused on what's important. When you're hungry for that one thing, that single element, whatever it is, it's astounding what you can achieve! And when you dedicate yourself to your cause, no matter the outcome, you can be proud that no one, no one on this planet, did what you did. You earned it. Against all odds, you did what you had to do.

I believe those who have faced situations entirely alone, without assistance, with nothing more than absolute determination, not only dealt with those particular issues, but they became better off *for themselves* and used the specific situations as stepping-stones to achieve what mattered most to them. I recommend that if needed, if possible, get help and guidance. Receive consolation. Think about the issue. Look at all of your options. Get a good night's sleep before making a decision. However, in the end it is *you* and you alone who have to *do* whatever it takes to accomplish your goal. Not your teacher, your parents, those at work, your spiritual leader, close friends, spouse, master motivator, guru, or psychic advisors. It's you!

Resolve to Make Things Happen for You

I mean no disrespect to anyone, but I have known many people who seemingly wake up with the idea of what they want and throw up their hands demanding that others do it for them in a right-now attitude. Maybe it's a learned behavior from years ago. That would explain why there are so many who seem so unable or unwilling to do for themselves. When I work with tough teenagers who feel that, for whatever reason, they cannot climb out of their situation, I ask them a series of questions: "If you are capable of getting dressed, going to the bathroom, and nuking something to eat in the microwave, then aren't you are old enough and capable enough to *do for yourself*?"

Years ago when my son, Stephen, turned ten, as we were talking about how proud I was of him and how far he had come, I said something that seemed to resonate within him. "Stephen," I stated, "you're ten years old now. You know right from wrong, good from evil, and the repercussions of your actions. I will always help you as best as I can. But realize this: From this moment on, you are a young man. And as a young man, understand that I can only help you so far."

Make this sentence your daily axiom, stating it aloud: "Whatever/whoever can only help me so far, can only do so much for me." It's like the old proverb, It is better to teach someone how to fish than to fish for them. As individuals, as a generation, as a society, and as a nation, I believe we need to be more responsible and rely more on ourselves. *At the end of the day those in our lives can only help us so far.*

Yes, it *may* seem impossible or hard to do, but when there is something that you want, that one thing you crave, ask yourself this: *How badly do I want it?* If your desire is that great, if it burns deep inside of you, day in and day out, then *you* will most likely find a way to make it happen.

This in no way means that you need some insurmountable challenge in your life to know what you want. Some have always known their desires; others one day out of the blue get that little idea that sprouts up within them. I am not saying you have to endure a gargantuan calamity to achieve success; yet I have found that when situations happen, whether big or small, *that's* when folks become more focused on what truly matters to them. When situations suddenly arise—whether problems with health, marriage, finances, work, college studies—in those everyday things that we take for granted, *that's* when we harness our motivation not only to overcome that one situation, but to ensure we are not likely to be in that dilemma ever again.

Years ago I read an article about the Air Florida plane crash and how some of the passengers were dying of hypothermia because they were unable to swim across the Potomac River. Because of the extreme conditions, the rescue team was limited as to what they could do to save those clinging for their lives. One such man who was freezing to death told himself he had two options: stay where he was and die, or at least try to swim across that river filled with large chunks of frozen ice. With every stroke this man imagined his wife and children. This brave individual not only overcame while focusing on what mattered most to him, but was able to save the lives of others who were either too terrified or unable to save themselves. This man, who before the event was criticized by his wife for being overly stoic and for not spending a great deal of time with his children, because of that event now beams with pride whenever he's at a family gathering and adores his wife, treating her like a princess. In a statement he later said that the plane crash was his wake-up call. With every day he knows he's living on borrowed time and intends to make the most of it.

Another story of overcoming is that of a young lady who ran for the track team in high school. She told me she knew that she wasn't the fastest person on the course and always felt defeated when others sprinted past her. One afternoon she exploded with a burst of energy and finished far ahead of the others. Afterward she confessed, "Even though I finished every race, in my mind I knew it was over whenever the other runners passed me. I just went through the motions. Today, I kept saying: one more kick, one more step, just one more. I wanted first place like never before. I gave it all I had and left nothing in reserve."

When there is something you long for, give it everything you have. How do you know what you are capable of unless you give it your all? Not halfway, but all the way. Not half speed, but full speed. You have a choice: you can freeze in that river or swim across and live life. You can halfheartedly run that race knowing all along that you will probably lose, or you can give it your all! Don't you quit on what's important to you. Don't give up on yourself! Again, I ask the question: Don't you deserve better?

Self-Respect

You may not even realize or may have forgotten that you already have accomplished a great deal in your life. Again, the smallest things can make a world of difference. And a little bit of struggle is not a bad thing. Take a moment. Ask yourself, without emotion, without a sulking attitude, what have you accomplished? Now, if your instantaneous reply is "Nothing!" you're not being fair to yourself, and you wouldn't be reading this book unless you took yourself seriously. So, what have you accomplished? Now, how did you do it? Whatever the situation, you most likely didn't have someone like a coach on the sidelines giving you the play-by-play game plan. It's not like you can throw up your hand and yell, "Hey, Ref, time out!" The truth of the matter is *you* simply did what you had to do. To meet that objective, short term or long term, whatever it was, *you* addressed that situation, took some responsibility, some action, a little bit of moxie, and gave it your best. If you didn't give it your all, next time do better. And you may have had butterflies in your stomach or you might have been a little scared, but *you* did it.

Give yourself some credit. Be grateful for yourself. Because of what you experienced and the challenges you addressed, are you not at least a little bit better off than before? A little stronger inside? A wee bit wiser? Do you find that when push comes to shove, you're a little more focused? A little more determined? Overall, because of what you've been through, do you realize what your true desires are? Then, stay on track and keep applying yourself. Even if you answer yes to only one of these questions, give yourself the credit you deserve, and instead of contaminating yourself by saying what you can't do, ask yourself *what* can you not accomplish when you truly commit to that one thing?

This is why I have the highest respect for hardworking single parents—both moms and dads—who bust their tails not only to provide for their kids, but to ensure that their children have at least a chance at a better life. And those with disabilities who—without any thought of being down-in-the-mouth or wasting their time and energy worrying how unfair life is—are far more upbeat and do far more than those who are so-called "without disabilities." I have the highest respect for anybody who, win or lose, feast or famine, knows what she wants and at least tries, even if it's against all odds, to better herself. As a country we root for the underdog, the Rocky Balboas, who step into the ring only to get beaten senseless by that overwhelming opponent, but yet the Rocky Balboas somehow find that inner strength to get up for the next round and give it their all. That's life. Win or lose, you take a few hits, you fall down, but when you get up from the mat, battered and bruised, you brush yourself off, tap into that inner drive, and give it what you've got. *That's* what counts.

In America all of us, every single one of us, from all walks of life, under the best and the worst of circumstances, has at least a chance of achieving, of fulfilling his or her desires. When you have a passion for that one thing, at times you have to go beyond the pain, the loneliness, frustration, even humiliation. You just do what you have to do.

As morbid as this may sound, not a single day passes that I do not look back at the time I was burned on the gas stove, starved for days, or anything else that happened to me, and have an odd sense of appreciation for at least having tried to learn something from the experience to better myself, to do something positive for myself. If I had the opportunity I would not change one moment of one day of my life. Not one! My experiences enabled me to become stronger inside, independent, and determined to make something out of myself. My challenges gave me a different perspective on life and made me want it more. To quote the international best-selling author of *The Christmas Box* and one of the most compassionate people I know, Richard Paul Evans, "It is in the darkest skies that the stars are best seen."

Discovering Your One Thing

So now that we are well versed on challenge, sacrifice, and resilience, let's get to the core of the issue: What do *you* want? I am not talking short-term goals or long-range, five-to-ten-year master plans; rather what is that singular thing that you desire? Now if you find yourself stumped, don't get discouraged; a majority of folks have no idea of what they want out of life. In fact, I have read several periodicals that claim as many as seventy percent of Americans haven't given it much thought, that most folks just live day by day, with few hopes or ambitions. Personally I think that's sad. Especially when we think of immigrants who have, even to this day, gone to great lengths, to the point of risking their own lives, just to *live* in America. Did you know that they have four to five times a better chance of reaching their goals, of achieving financial success, of fulfilling their dreams, for the simple fact that they have always known what they wanted and were determined to make it happen? How many people do you know who roll out of bed, go through the motions, drag themselves to school, or make their living doing "whatever," day in and day out, thinking to themselves that this is as good as life gets? I am not implying that everyone jump up and plan every aspect of their lives down to the second, but shouldn't we at least apply ourselves and utilize our gifts to our fullest potential?

Sometimes when I address an audience, I ask the question: "What do you want?" I then recommend for them—whether they are business professionals or everyday private citizens—to spend time and "purge" on paper everything they desire. Everything! This alone would take hours. Because of this, I advise folks to list specific categories their "wants" would fall into: health, family, spirituality, education, business, finances, interpersonal relationships, personal desires; whatever it is that may be important to that person. Next, I have the person pick a category, find the first item in that category, and compare it to their next and without hesitation check off what they want out of the two. Then, compare the first item to the third item and instantly place a check mark next to the choice made, followed by the first item to the fourth, and so on, until all the items have been ranked against the first one. Next, I have the audience compare the second item on their list with the third item, then the second item with the fourth and so on. All the items on the list will be ranked against the others and value-graded accordingly by that person's desires, with a check mark.

If you do this exercise, I ask you to do it exactly as just explained, and without apprehension or pretense. Lower your defenses and invest some absolute quality time in yourself and you will discover something amazing. The things you thought were *so* important—that new car, office promotion, acing that test, losing a few pounds, "getting" that "new thing" for your home—are way, way down on your list of priorities of what you really, truly want.

As highly as I recommend this exercise, and as imperative as it is for you to bare your soul to yourself, if you wish to cut to the chase I can save you a great deal of time. I have found over the years the unequivocal "thing" that folks want out of life is: TO BE HAPPY!! That's it! Feast or famine, rain or shine, good days or bad, happiness is what nearly all of us want out of life. When we're happy does it truly matter how much we have, what people think of us, or what we look like? When you are happy with who you are and what you have in your life right now, isn't everything else a bonus? How many weddings have you attended where you see that look of love in the bride's and groom's eyes but know they have a long road ahead of them? That they may live in a hole-in-the-wall rundown apartment, with limited furnishings, and both working full-time jobs just to make ends meet? And yet, when they're together, the world stops for them. Being with each other is all they need.

In just about every situation I have been exposed to—whether flying combat support missions during the War in the Gulf or working nonstop for days on end while not seeing my family for weeks at a time—I've tried my best to maintain a positive attitude. Maybe all that I have endured in the past has made it easier for me to find something optimistic about either my surroundings or whatever I had to deal with at that particular time. During the War in the Gulf, while thousands of service members lived in tents and ate food from a tube, I was fortunate enough to receive one hot meal a day and take a shower with hot water. I was happy and appreciative. As a presenter, at times when I've pushed myself beyond my normal boundaries, I've become energized about the opportunity of "just one more program"—then afterward I will reward myself and relax with a simple cup of coffee. I grab or sometimes "steal" a few moments alone outside, a few hours reading a book—just a little bit of happiness anywhere, anytime, I can. It's not easy and I may rant and complain as much as the next person; however, as much as I apply myself in whatever I do, I now apply that same amount of energy and focus in doing *something* for myself that enables me to feel from deep within just a little bit better.

So, if being happy ranks number one, did you know that the second most important thing is love and/or acceptance? As you know, once we feel secure in ourselves and among others, this not only enables us to face all the better the challenges that may be in store for us, but being accepted is one of the main needs we have as human beings. When I worked in juvenile hall, I had the chance to work with teens who would join gangs. The main reasons they did so were for "love" and a "family"-like acceptance.

Next on the list, immediately after love and/or acceptance, is their children's prosperity, or for those who do not have children it's health for themselves and others they care for. After happiness, love/acceptance, health/prosperity, this "List of Life" varies. But in my years of assisting others and the stories I have read or people I have had the privilege to meet, these are what truly resonate within just about all of us on a continual basis.

I've found "the things" that folks thought were so important, so imperative—fame, fortune, weight loss, hair gain—were way, way, way down the list. I'm not surprised. I cannot tell you how many people I know who *have* fame, fortune, stellar careers, immaculate bodies, *and* every, and I mean every, materialistic item the world can offer, and yet some of these folks are unfulfilled, insecure, and absolutely miserable. While I believe one shouldn't judge those who live in a fishbowl world—as none of us truly knows what these people have been through or what they gave up in order to achieve their status—I'd rather be grounded and appreciative of the everyday "little things" in life. How many movies have you seen in which the main characters crave escaping small-town USA to make something of themselves in search of fame and fortune? The characters push themselves past normal limits, take a few hard knocks, then finally break through and receive everything they longed for and have the world in the palm of their hand, yet still feel so hollow, so incomplete. In the end they discover they have lost themselves in the process of their quest and would give up everything just to live a "normal life."

Invest in Yourself

Sit down, spend some quality time with yourself, and discover from the deepest recesses of your heart *what is truly important to you*. Find it. Hold on to it. Live it. No matter how hard it may be, keep a positive attitude. Don't take setbacks personally. Look at them as opportunities to see what you're truly made of. Never lose sight of your objective. But *please* don't lose yourself in the process. Don't be too hard on yourself, for you will fall down; yet it is getting up that truly matters. Find something, do something, every single day that brings you one step closer to your goal and reward yourself for your valiant efforts, no matter how insignificant they may seem. *Be happy within yourself and what you have right now, every single day.* Find that solace within yourself, for anything else can only make things better.

HELP YOURSELF REMINDERS

* DEFINING MOMENTS OR SITUATIONS CAN BE A POSITIVE CATALYST AS *THE* TURNING POINT IN YOUR LIFE.
* BEFORE YOU QUIT ON YOURSELF WHEN LIFE ISN'T FAIR, EXHAUST ALL YOUR OPTIONS FOR MAKING THINGS HAPPEN.
* IF YOU WANT IT, YOU HAVE TO MAKE IT POSSIBLE.
* WHEN FIGHTING TO MAKE YOUR LIFE BETTER, GIVE YOURSELF THE CREDIT YOU DESERVE.
* TAKE THE TIME AND ENERGY TO TRULY INVEST IN YOUR MOST IMPORTANT ASSET: YOURSELF.

5

The Price You Pay

Knowing what you want out of life is critical, but it's not enough to make your dreams come true. As you know, just because you long for something or even have a dying passion for that one thing does not mean you will automatically obtain it. I believe when it comes to fulfilling your dreams there is always a price you must pay.

In the preceding chapter I deliberately went into specific detail about how I had feared for my life. The price I paid to stay alive was being attacked by my mother. That day I lost a lot of blood and my face felt like a punching bag, but the expense was not only worth it to me but it became my foundation for survival. In the end it always comes down to how badly you really, truly want it.

While there are a great many folks who *think* they know what they want, many are unwilling to apply even the smallest amount of effort to obtain their goals.

For years our country has become a culture of "quick fix." Words like *sacrifice, diligence,* and *honor* no longer matter and have been replaced with *I want it all and I want it now!* Relationships flourish and dissolve faster than paint can dry. Some see that flashy sports car and they want it. They cannot afford it but it doesn't matter, for they have to have it now! With a quick scribble on a check, the car they have been dreaming of for ten minutes is suddenly theirs. But when the payment comes due, suddenly that thing they wanted isn't all that appealing as it was a few months ago. Emotions become involved, egos get bruised, and it's always the other guy's fault when the car is repossessed. I've seen the same in the job market. With only a few weeks of experience under their belts, some people tell others how the task should be performed, that they don't *have* to do such and such, and are the first to complain about every single thing, while the entire time they barely apply themselves to the job; and yet they are the ones who become extremely agitated when they are not promoted to a management position after being with the company for an earth-shattering six weeks.

Another approach society has is: if things don't turn out, we can always sue. In this day and age we can file lawsuits for mental duress, loss of sleep, coffee being too hot or too cold, and even air turbulence when flying. Years ago I read where a prison inmate sued the state because the mattress hurt his back, and another inmate sued because he slipped and fell on the wet floor. And when folks complain how justice is slower than a snail, part of the reason for that is today's courts spend a great deal of time tied up in frivolous lawsuits. I have the staunchest belief in justice. I believe in equal treatment for one and all, yet every day we can pick up the paper and read how Mr. So-and-So is attempting to collect millions over something that seems entirely ridiculous.

It Doesn't Happen Overnight

Maybe it's me, but as a society haven't we become just a bit too cynical? While some folks spend a great deal of time and energy plotting the next quick-fix, get-rich, have-it-all-right-now scheme, the reality is they would be better off applying their time and energy in more proven conventional areas—studying hard, applying themselves at their craft, sacrificing a little, praying they get lucky—for there are no quick fixes. Unless you hit Lotto, and that's only after you called one of the psychic hotlines to receive the exact numbers, there is no such thing as an overnight success. Remember the old saying If it sounds to good to be true it probably is? If you doubt me, turn on your television any time after 2:00 A.M., flip to the infomercials, and find the so-called expert who is so excited that he is on the verge of exploding into your home because, "Now, right now, I've got something so incredible, so earth shattering, that—that . . . I can't put it into words! But I can tell *you*! I just discovered something that will change your life. . . . But you have to act now! For a limited time only, I am making *you* a one-time offer. . . ."

This person implores you to listen to his patented, foolproof, instant results, super-duper, hundred-percent-guaranteed secret, ". . . just so you, *my dear friend,* can have it all, *right now,* at the amazing low low price of . . ." And it's gotta be true, for you see the endless testimonials of couples who were on the brink of oblivion and are now living the good life. And in the early-morning hours everything makes sense and looks good—the fleet of fancy cars, the breathtaking mansion, the streamlined race boats, the helicopters, the luscious bikini-clad smiling models who somehow can't keep their hands off of our newfound savior. With only a few hours of sleep under my belt this makes perfect sense to me. If it works for the host and *all* those people, and if I can see all that stuff with my own eyes, then it's gotta be true!

I know of many professionals who are truly sincere in helping others, but, hello! Reality check! Not to sound selfish or stoic, but think of it this way: If you had a secret that you had recently discovered, would *you* hawk your discovery on late-night TV for the entire world? In the same vein, I know many who have confessed to me that they fear so many people coming after them if they ever came into a great deal of money, that aside from their spouse and maybe their children, they wouldn't tell a soul.

The funny thing is after all these years and the countless overnight experts who have promised the world and in the end have had their businesses shut down, some indicted, and some of them jailed, there are still those who are desperately looking for "the next big thing."

I am not trying to limit your options or discourage you from exploring your boundaries; for if you truly believe in something that strongly, then by all means go for it. However, the cold hard truth is if you make it overnight—if you get the girl, the boy, the money, the car, the whatever—you can lose it just as fast. When you give it a great deal of thought with a clear head and discover your one desire, the truth is there: it's not going to happen overnight.

Absolute Devotion

Just a few years ago, immediately after Tiger Woods won the Masters in Augusta, Georgia, everyone bombarded him. I read how one person asked Tiger, "Son, what's it like to pick up a golf club and start whacking those balls as well as you do?" Tiger, who I believe is one of America's positive role models for all ages, smiled and replied, "Sir, I've been hitting balls for about nineteen years." "Nineteen years?!" the older man exclaimed, "Son, how old are you?" Again smiling, Tiger answers, "Twenty-one, sir."

Think about it: when Tiger was a toddler, his father, Earl, would teach him how to hold a putter, swing a club, address the ball, and sink a putt. Every day, Tiger played golf. Every day. I've read about how, when Tiger was still in elementary school, he would memorize golf courses, plotting every hit with specific clubs. Tiger devoted his time and efforts to his art. He sacrificed a lot in the process, but paid the price to achieve his greatness.

To get a little, you have to be willing to give up a lot.

The Tonight Show talk show host Jay Leno took a lot of flack when he received the slot as the host for the television show. Countless people wrote the network claiming that since they didn't know who this "new" comedian was, obviously Jay didn't deserve the coveted job; that Jay was simply a product of being recently discovered. Now, even though I am a huge David Letterman fan, I must give Mr. Leno his due. After reading Leno's book, *Leading with My Chin,* I learned that it took Jay fifteen years to become an overnight success. Day in and day out, Jay worked in strip bars, condemned rooms, practically every college campus, every day for years. What made him different from other comics was that Jay's approach was humble, straightforward, and clean, while relating to his audience on everyday experiences. At the time, he had racked up so many air miles that he was considered to have more frequent flier miles than anyone else in the United States!

Work hard, study your craft, get lucky.

Years ago, I knew a young woman named Mary who as an ice skater was yearning to make the Olympics. She would get up at three-thirty in the morning, have her father drive her to the ice rink at four, skate nonstop for over two and a half hours, shower, grab a quick bite, attend a full day of school, and work part-time. *Then* after eight in the evening, Mary would again skate for another two hours, only to return home exhausted, but feeling fulfilled that she had given it her all. Astonished, years later I asked Mary how in the world was she even able to do half of all she did. "I never saw it that way. I knew if I were to stand a chance [of making the Olympics], I was going to have to give it my all and dig deep. Seeing all those beautiful princesses gliding on the ice was so inspiring to a young girl. Every day and every night I wanted to be like one of them! My room was covered with posters of Peggy Fleming and Dorothy Hamill. They were the first thing I saw in the morning and the last thing I saw at night. And even though I didn't make the cut, it was one of the most fulfilling times of my life. No one took anything away from me because I gave it my all. To this day whenever I tackle something, all I do is reach back to where I was back then as a teenager."

Now, there's a person who has earned the right to complain that all her time, efforts, and sacrifices didn't pay off. But Mary, like most of us, realized even with the best of intentions, even if you pay the price, there are no guarantees to achievement. You can give it your all, climb that mountain against all odds, and *still* come up just short of your well-deserved goal. With all my heart I do wish I could tell you differently. Yet as for Mary's endeavor, she was able to take something away from her experiences that no one could give her: humility and self-fulfillment.

While a lot of people see someone like Mr. Leno deliver a hilarious monologue that *seems* so off the cuff or a skater like Mary give a flawless performance on ice, they have little idea of the resolve it took, the sacrifices made, or how many times both people fell flat on their faces, just for Jay and Mary to reach the bottom rung of the ladder of success. Most of us only see the finished product, forgetting entirely the immense work involved.

Tiger, Jay, and Mary all applied themselves, but *not* for the sole quest of glory, but rather for the glimmer of hope of achieving their desires. Again, just for the chance of achieving success. The lesson is, whether staying home an extra half hour studying for a test, doing additional research for a project at work, or just being there for that one person you love, somehow make your venture an everyday part of your life so it won't seem as much a monumental effort on your part.

The Boundless Optimist

When I think of one person who paid the price of hard work with constant enthusiasm as an everyday lifestyle, the name Arnold Schwarzenegger comes to mind. After years of extensive planning and barely out of his teens Arnold broke the status quo by not only moving away from his small village of Thal, but leaving his country of Austria with the sole objective of making it in America. Totally out of his element and with nothing more than a few dollars in his pockets, Arnold arrived in America seeing only the vast opportunities that lay before him. While most of America *discovered* Arnold in his earlier B films, he had *already* conquered the world of body building by winning an unprecedented seven Mr. Olympia titles. It is said that Arnold would work out four hours in the morning, then another four hours in the afternoon. While some of us gripe about putting in eight hours a day for our jobs, Arnold would make his workouts his vocation, lifting, curling, pressing tons of weights, eight hours a day! During the same time period, struggling to understand and comprehend the English language, he attended college six hours a day, working on two different degrees at the same time. If that weren't enough, in order to feed himself and maintain his sparse apartment, Arnold, with his friend Franco Columbo, worked late into the evening until the early morning hours as masons at their own business called Pumping Bricks, six hours a day. When you add the time involved, that's twenty hours a day, every day, for years on end.

When researching articles written about Mr. Schwarzenegger, I discovered how baffled folks were by his drive. How in the world could someone like Arnold accomplish so much, so fast, when folks like you and me, who have lived in America all of our lives, become so pessimistic? Answer: unyielding determination. While others badmouthed every situation they were in, how tough or unfair life was, how all the opportunities were used up, Arnold pressed forward with nothing more than pure optimism. He actually enjoyed every challenge that came his way.

Arnold's phenomenal success was not without enormous setbacks. Knowing full well a career as a body builder was limited, as a child Arnold had already set his eyes on acting; but when he arrived in America some agents and producers went out of their way to belittle Arnold, that as a body builder he obviously lacked intelligence, his body was too big for the screen, his German accent too thick, and even his name too long for the marquee. Arnold not only deflected every obstacle with his charming quick wit, but he applied himself even more. Becoming a relentless self-promoter, Arnold would *inform* practically anyone he met that he was destined to succeed, thus becoming one of the biggest draws in the film business and one of the most recognized names in the world. Today, Arnold lends his limited free time traveling throughout the nation at his own expense to some of the country's toughest inner-city schools, promoting health, physical fitness, and more importantly, challenging the younger generation to strive to better themselves.

Constant Application

Again, there is no such thing as an overnight success. Period. If there is one key to success, one key to obtaining your desires, then it's one word: Work. Work, work, work, work, work. In everything you do, apply yourself. Like all these individuals we've discussed, or anyone else for that matter, harness your ambitions, be enthusiastic, and dedicate yourself to your cause.

Don't be alarmed. I'm not looking to frighten anyone and I'm not endorsing a workaholic mentality. Absolutely not. But, what if your mind-set was to accomplish your objective with seemingly little effort, and it merely became a part of your everyday routine? How do you do something that seems so overwhelming? You do a little here and a little there until your overwhelming, arduous, impossible challenges become your everyday routine. In a nutshell, that's it.

Think of it as a baby learning to walk. As simple as it may seem for most of us, to me the act of walking, or anything else that involves motor function, is nothing short of extraordinary. The brain has to think it, and relay to the body where to go and the speed of the stride; all within a fraction of a millisecond. So how do most of us learn to walk? First and foremost we have to process a desire to do so. We stand up, we wobble a few times because we're unsure of the new experience. Maybe we have a little apprehension, but that's okay, for our ambition kicks in. We take a step, maybe two, then unexpectedly we fall down. Sometimes on our padded behind, sometimes flat on our face. It hurts, it's not fair, sometimes we cry, but we get up; we still have that drive to move forward. For some babies, you can see that pure excitement in their eyes with each foot placed in front of the other, until suddenly, without thinking, these kids are tearing up the house running away from frantic parents who are trying to put them in the bathtub! Wow!

And yet, the act of walking was performed without government assistance, with no one to prosecute when the toddlers fell down, or no one to complain to if Mommy, Daddy, or any other person tricked the young tyke by taking a step or two backward so baby could walk just a few more steps on her own, before being caught in the arms of the one who helped her along the way.

When we are willing to pay the price, when we carry that desire deep within our heart that no one or any situation can take away from us, are there truly any excuses? In every article I have read, among people I have been privileged to interview, the ones who accomplished something significant to themselves, against enormous odds, all, one way or another, have had the same philosophy: *They wanted it more and were willing to pay the price it took to achieve their desires.*

When San Francisco Giants pitcher Dave Dravecky discovered he had cancer in his pitching arm, through tremendous pain, and placing his health at extreme risk, he fought back to pitch yet again before the disease got the best of his arm, which eventually was amputated. Because of his belief that all races are equal, Nelson Mandela was a political prisoner for over twenty-five years, subjected to torture, mock executions, and isolation. Willing to lay down his life for a better nation, Mr. Mandela not only survived but became the president of South Africa. As a teenager Michael Jordan didn't make the cut for his high-school basketball team, so he resolved to practice for hours on end every single day. Years later, in 1997 during a critical playoff game and while suffering from the stomach flu, through sheer intensity and fighting off overwhelming coverage from the opposing team, Mr. Jordan tapped back into the time when he'd wanted nothing more than to play basketball. That day Michael's commitment was so great that immediately after the closing buzzer of the game, he physically collapsed into the arms of his teammate Scottie Pippen. When U.S. Air Force F-16 pilot Captain Scott O'Grady was shot down while flying a mission over Bosnia, desperate to avoid capture by those searching for him literally inches away, he not only survived by eating bugs for over six days, but was even careful of how he breathed so his would-be captors could not hear him or see the cold white mist escape from his mouth.

In all instances these brave individuals longed for that *one thing* and were more than willing to forfeit whatever it took to reach their goals. You and I are no different. We simply have to make that commitment to make it happen.

Don't Give Your Best Away

We all have desires. On any given day in our lives. And I believe all of us have the best of intentions. Especially young minds. I *know* you do, otherwise you would not be spending your valuable time and brain cells digesting this book. But the reality is that we give our best away. No one takes it from us; we give it away. *We* do—not the government, our parents, our past, our boss, our spouse, the floods, hurricanes, tornadoes, high tide, solar eclipse . . . whatever. We quit. We have wants, needs, we *try* to make a go of it, or maybe we do just enough to get by. We allow time, situations, or whatever else to erode our dreams. We quit on ourselves. We carry regret, regret turns into frustration, frustration into anger, anger into sorrow. And all the while life has slipped away from us . . . one day, one grain of sand, at a time. In the end, we look into the mirror and we can't even recognize that person staring back at us. We've lost one of life's most precious gifts: the excitement, the fear, the heart-pounding sensation of taking a step outside our protective womb. Just a step, or two, into the unknown. Sometimes in the blink of an eye to get that quick fix, or in a moment of frustration, anger, self-doubt, or weakness we give up our desire to do *something* to better ourselves.

And all you have to do is *apply yourself*.

As I confessed before, I despise writing. It takes me forever to write a halfway decent, semi-intelligent sentence. I lack patience, my brain goes a million miles a minute, I have limited mechanics, and cannot type to save my life. Years ago I was inspired by something that famed author of over 150 Western novels, Louis L'Amour, once said—something like "At times, when I can't think of a thing to write, I commit myself to writing just one sentence a day. One sentence. Sometimes that one sentence will lead to two, and soon I'm on a roll."

Work, work, work, work. Whether it's your marriage, interpersonal relationships, raising kids, your health, schooling, or your career, apply yourself. When it comes to relationships, I think a lot of us unknowingly take the other person for granted. Remember when "that person" was all you thought about, almost as if you were possessed? No matter how bad your day was, when you thought of him/her, your day was just a little bit better.

But now that you've been together all this time, you may feel like "Yeah, we're still in love, I guess, but, uh . . ." I don't care how long you've been together, or how many struggles you've endured, how deep, secure, head over heels you *think* your love is, don't take your institution for granted. When was the last time you applied yourself to your relationship? When was the last time you just held hands as you sat outside alone together, gave that person a ten-second kiss or a thirty-second hug? Before you answer, just stop for a moment, close your eyes, and think. Think about it. *The person I'm with today can leave me tomorrow.*

When it comes to children, all of us just ogle over every little thing babies do—the things they try to stick in their mouths, the way they drool on themselves, even the first time they fill their Pampers. But, after the first ten to fourteen years, the kids . . . well, they lose that "cuteseyness." Totally. Especially those teenagers who come home with a body tattoo that reads "All access here." So how did we lose that "ogleness"? Complacency, overriding priorities, or it may be that as parents we believe we've already raised them to know right from wrong, how to make decisions for themselves, and we grant them independence, as they start to push for it. A couple of years ago I read a report from the American Medical Association, on the subject of child psychology, that stressed preteens and teenagers require just as much time, attention, and guidance as babies. All of us know the importance of a proper diet and exercise to maintain our health. Regarding education, don't rest too much on your past—it doesn't matter how good a grade you received on that test yesterday, but what you can discern and be graded upon today. There is so much to learn. Continue to apply yourself. Remember: knowledge is power. The same goes for sports: you're only as good as your last game. In the corporate world I've seen those who get so pumped up about that new job opportunity and how they've poured everything they had into the interview; what they wore, how they walked, sat, how they responded to each and every question, but after a while the exuberance erodes and the output slackens, therefore lessening their chances of climbing that career ladder of success.

All I'm trying to stress in all these illustrations is the importance of not becoming too complacent, that's all. With all that you are able to do, apply a little extra, just an extra nudge, every day, and see the difference it makes in your attitude and the outcome of your achievements.

Again, it will take some effort on your part *and* your world will not change overnight, but think of it in this light: with that additional push you're giving, things can only get better. I think a lot of us rush into some things without having the faintest idea of what in the hell we're doing, why we're so intent on doing it, let alone the sacrifices it will take to get us there. Not to be too judgmental, but an example that stands out is that of the been-there-done-that corporate individual I once read about who joined an expedition to climb Mount Everest. Without all the necessary training and self-reliance required, this individual nearly died by stupidly pushing too hard, not listening to experienced guides when needed, and packing so many needless items—such as gourmet food, a portable TV with video player, hoards of computer equipment including a satellite phone—that it took four expert Sherpas to carry them. All this just to boast of filing dispatches via the Internet from the top of Mount Everest. For all this person's lofty goals, such as they may have been, others had to expend their precious energy while placing their own well-being at risk, and had to *assist* this person down from the summit.

Practical, Obtainable Objectives

Some of us take on too much or attempt to tackle our objectives too fast. I think part of the problem stems from our setting outrageous, unattainable goals, thus setting ourselves up for failure, which can leave us feeling more defeated than we were beforehand. That's why I become so irritated when I hear of individuals who are taken advantage of by some of these late-night infomercial saviors of the universe.

I recommend small, bite-sized, just-beyond-reach kinds of goals that can be fulfilled on a daily basis. Years ago, before serving in the air force, I sold cars for a living. Because there were over forty salespeople scrambling over each other in every which way they could for a possible sale, I quickly learned not only what to do, but more importantly, what *not* to do. While a majority of the sales force would thrust their business cards at every customer who drove onto the lot before sprinting off to give another card to another person, I would spend time with each and every potential client. I freely admit that most of the time I did not sell a lot of vehicles. However, there were many times when I was fortunate enough to be the only salesman at the dealership that day to sell not just one but two cars.

Whenever I speak at sales conferences, I stress the same ideology. In this hypersonic, information-runs-the-universe, *press-one-for-further-options*-just-so-you-can-speak-to-a-machine type of virtual world, I think we are losing that authentic face-to-face personal service. So many people are so busy chasing their tails, they forget that these things man invented were to make our lives easier. I see so many brilliant businesspeople, particularly in the sales force, wasting their time and energy, and at the end of the day they've accomplished little to nothing that improved their overall position. Case in point: For a few days I shadowed a salesman who would literally give you a card, e-mail address, and pager number if you, whatever your name is, have any questions, before racing off to meet another "client," before dashing to attend a meeting, then another, then another, until he saw one more "client." At the end of the day I asked this salesman, "What did you accomplish?" "Look," he proudly showed me, "I got all these business leads!" Thinking to myself, I calculated that he spent about three minutes per "client." He was so busy rushing to rush that I didn't think it was worth the energy he expended. "No, you don't," I replied to the salesman. "You've got cards with names, addresses, and phone numbers." "Aha!" laughed the salesman, "That's where you're wrong. These are great leads. You watch when I follow up on them. . . ." This gentleman that I had spent the day with was truly a nice fellow, and he was so proud that I almost didn't have the heart, but I felt I had to do it. He chuckled at me about his "leads" right up until the moment I opened his glove box, which literally spilled with "leads" accumulated over the past few months.

My friend somehow got so caught up grabbing every lead he could as his short-term goal, he forgot about spending some time on his customers' needs in order to sell his product. All I advised was for him to pay the price of spending his time and focusing his entire attention on one client at a time. Build that relationship. Fill that pipeline. In business or even in more personal matters, if you made a good contact in the morning, hey, you're on a roll; go for another one that afternoon. Don't worry about what you might be missing; focus on what you may have right now. When dealing with a mass market, that's the price you pay. In a sense, you have to kiss a lot of frogs until you come across that prince.

The same goes for those I know who battle with weight. They want to lose all those unsightly pounds and have that beautiful body . . . right now! First of all, that's not going to happen. No one gains weight overnight and I don't believe we can lose it overnight either. Secondly, you don't want to *lose* weight, you want to *get rid* of it.

Think of it in these terms: When you lose your keys, you find them. When you ditch that bad date, you hope he/she doesn't turn up. You don't want to wake up one day to discover that the weight you "lost" found your thighs or abdominal area, do you? Now, you could pay the price and take a chance at trying every "just-discovered-from-the-far-reaches-of-an-ancient-society," "herbal," "organic," "safe-for-all-ages," "fun-for-the-whole-family" diet. Or, you can even literally exercise yourself to death. Another option: You can watch and weigh every gram of fat, analyze protein versus carbohydrates all you want, but do you really want to live that type of life, *every single day*? Certain athletes and models certainly do, and it's not all that it's cracked up to be. But again that's the price they pay. I'm sure Mr. Schwarzenegger every so often indulges in a piece of strudel; or supermodel X probably sneaks a slice of pizza every once in a while. But to do all that, to put yourself through so much in the hopes that *you'll like yourself* more or *others will notice you*, is it worth it? Especially for women who battle with issues of low esteem that are placed upon them in part by society. Like my friend, who I swear looks like a skeleton but has brainwashed herself into thinking she is overweight and fears her husband will leave her if she wears anything more than a size two. Knowing this lady as I do, I think it is more about an unresolved issue of self-esteem and fear of abandonment, than her physical appearance.

From what I know, human beings have several different body structures and there is only so much you can do with any specific form. And if you're basically happy with the one you have and are in good health, I would hate for you or someone you may know to go through all the time and anguish of trying to change it, if it's really not going to make all that much of a difference. I know so many folks who do lose a great deal of weight, but those yo-yo diets mean just that—they will gain back what they lost, if not more, when the yo-yo comes back up. The sad part is those extreme diets can actually do more harm than good, not only on that person's esteem but it places a tremendous amount of stress on that person's heart. So, is it truly worth the cost?

Believe me, I'm one for physical fitness. I watch what I eat and have a set exercise routine so I can live a long productive life. However, I'm not going to have my life dictated with worry of trying to have this imaginary chiseled body that in reality I can never have. That doesn't mean that I'm some couch potato. Nobody enjoys a slice of chocolate cheesecake and a frothy mocha more than me! But those who know me know that if I splurge, the next morning I start my day with an extra few sets with the weights and run an extra mile or two on the treadmill. I'm never going to have a rippling chest, twenty-inch arms, or washboard stomach. As I approach midlife, I'm content. I'm always looking for ways to improve my body so I can look good in that one shirt, but it's not the end of the world if I rarely wear shorts because I feel I have the legs of a chicken. I'm only human.

Keep Plugging Away

Even when people pay the price, a fair number of them expect instantaneous results and become upset that they didn't receive all they wanted. It's like anyone who's self-employed: there is a tremendous amount of sweat equity involved. Some folks say it takes a good business three to five years of scraping by just to build a good foundation. But there are many who become upset and throw up their hands because they are still, day in and day out, paying the price. I've known a few people in the music business who actually believed in their hearts that they would "make it overnight," but even after being given the opportunity they cut their music video, became disgruntled, and soon enough tempers flared until the band with the latest breakthrough sound finally broke up.

Renowned ice climber Yvon Chouinard became a blacksmith to invent the perfect ice ax for his fellow climbers. But even as Mr. Chouinard's reputation grew throughout the nation and parts of the globe as the only person at the time making unique equipment for climbers, Yvon had to sell his wares from the trunk of his dilapidated car, while surviving on game hunted in the nearby forest or on cans of cat food that he purchased by the case. With time, diligence, and immense sacrifice, Yvon Chouinard now has a fifty-million-dollar business selling what many consider the premier outdoor equipment in the world.

Some folks quit on themselves even though they're so close to achieving their goals. I had a friend, Don, who wanted to get rid of a hundred pounds. After taking control and persisting in his lifelong battle, Don, God bless him, got rid of sixty pounds, but after a run of bad luck at work and some problems at home, he felt like a loser and wanted to throw in the towel. "I'm never going to make it. I'm destined to be a loser. Look at me!" he cried.

"That's right!" I fired back. "Look at you. You're looking good, feeling better. This time last year you couldn't even walk around the block once, and now you're riding your mountain bike eight, ten miles a day. Maybe you've got a way to go, but *look at how much you've done*!"

When Don replied that getting rid of sixty pounds wasn't that much and complained how far he was from his goal, I gave him a pair of thirty-pound dumbbells. "Here," I said, "hold these for a while. Or better yet, tie them around your neck. Heavy, eh?" I smiled. "Now, *that's* how far you've come!"

Peaks and Valleys

Life is not now nor ever will be black and white. In Don's case, life pulled him a little off course. Just as with an airplane, sometimes a crosswind may blow us off course or we hit an unexpected air pocket and lose our altitude. Yet all we have to do is check our direction and make a slight adjustment to get where we want to go. To quote a friend of mine, Del Mearse, who knows about diligence and staying on course, and who is also in the top one percent of all chartered financial consultants in the United States: "Life is like walking up the stairs while playing yo-yo." Even when you're progressing, every once in a while you will hit some peaks and valleys. Every day you're working, you're studying, you're scrimping, you're saving, paying your dues, and *bam*: life just slaps you down on the mat. Again, it's not fair, it's not right, but what are you going to do about it? After all that you've done, all you've been through and now sacrificed for, don't you deserve better? My advice: brush yourself off, get up, and *go the distance*.

Pardon my language, but sometimes life just sucks. And even if you try to stay away from all those mud puddles, life's pool of muck will find you, no matter what you do. Some days you're on top of your game and can do no wrong, and other days, well, you would have been better off if you'd stayed in bed. And let's say you had a bad day and had a few bites of "Chunky Monkey" ice cream, or in a moment of weakness at the mall this pair of shoes or that power tool that you know you're never going to use screamed to you, "Take me home!" Big deal: so you spent a few bucks, you gained a whopping half a pound. It's not the end of the world.

Here's an exercise: Before you throw in the towel, before you become your own worst enemy ask yourself this: "Am I better off today than I was yesterday, last week, last month, or last year?" If the answer's yes, well then, keep on keeping on. Part of the thrill of success is the journey of the struggle. If it were easy, everyone would be doing it. The truth is you're probably on the downstroke of that yo-yo. Again, every day you're climbing that ladder of success, but you just hit some unexpected turbulence and lost a little bit of altitude. Don't cave in at the first sign of trouble. Before you even think about it, take a good sound look at where you were, where you're at now, and how close you are to achieving that one thing you've hungered for so long. The reality is you will fall down, but as always it's getting up that counts. That's the making of a successful person—someone who takes a few hits but is willing to accept them and more in order to pay the price. And if you quit now, all that you've fought for and forfeited would have been in vain. Personally, I can think of nothing sadder than a person who quits on herself.

So give yourself a little bit of credit for even attempting to accomplish something others wouldn't even consider. Every day, keep paying your dues and make a stride or two to bring yourself closer to your goal. Just be mindful of the road apples in your path. And when you step in one, scrape it off and continue your journey. Remember, everyone has setbacks. Half of Jay Leno's jokes are so bad, they should be flushed. As phenomenal as Tiger Woods is, he does not win every tournament. I once saw Michael Jordan on his last shot of his last game of his career, with only seconds left in the game, make the basket that won the Chicago Bulls their NBA championship. Afterward, as everyone praised Mr. Jordan for his concentration and for pulling through in the clutch, he smiled and said something like "Yeah, I got lucky. But do you know how many times I've blown the game because

I missed that exact same shot?" You're not going to succeed unless you try. And you will fail more than you succeed.

Even with the perfect master plan there is only so much under your control. But you will not get anywhere unless you know where you're going. And, in order to get there you have to be willing to give up something in return. The test of mettle is what you have endured that made the impossible possible. Before you quit, get a good night's sleep. Situations have a tendency to look different when you have all your perceptions in your corner. See how you feel. Regroup. Take a time out. Realize you may never get the golden ring. But are you better off now than you were just a little bit ago? For there are so many people pushing, striving for that one thing. *And having that one thing is great, but if you're not enough with it, you'll never be enough without it.*

HELP YOURSELF REMINDERS

* IF YOU CAN OBTAIN IT OVERNIGHT, YOU CAN LOSE IT JUST AS QUICKLY.

* DEVOTE YOURSELF EVERY DAY TO YOUR CAUSE.

* APPLY YOURSELF WITH ENTHUSIASM FOR WHAT YOU WILL ACCOMPLISH.

* ATTEMPT THE SO-CALLED "IMPOSSIBLE" UNTIL IT BECOMES AN EVERYDAY PART OF YOUR LIFE.

* No one takes anything away from us, unless we give up on ourselves first.

* When you hit that expected bump in the road, it's only a bump in the road.

Part Three

Celebrate Who You Are and What You Have

6

If It All Ended Tomorrow

As a kid, I had to make the most of my situation. Since I was about six, Mother had decided, for whatever reason, that I was no longer allowed the privilege of being a member of "the family," and was therefore banished to live in the garage. At first, surrounded by darkness, I was terrified of every little sound above and around me. I had thought for sure that some huge, hairy, five-eyed, demonic swamp monster or gigantic orange-red snake would emerge from underneath the car, an overhead water pipe, or from some water drain and either eat me alive or squeeze me to death. At first, if my imagination didn't get the best of me, the chilling dampness and the hard reality of exclusion depressed me all the more. The winters were the hardest, especially during the holiday season. As "the family" trimmed the tree, listened to Christmas records, or watched television specials, I stood at the base of the garage stairs, leaning my shoulders and the back of my neck against a beam of wood, with my eyes clamped shut, fantasizing I was somewhere else.

My days started and ended in the garage. Sleeping on an army cot that I used as my bed, I'd awake with a shred of hope of being fed breakfast. I'd push myself with lightning speed trying to complete my morning chores before sprinting off to school. Then, the moment school was dismissed, as conditioned I'd run home to perform Mother's endless list of afternoon chores, then either stand at the base of the garage stairs or sit on top of my hands on a bed of rocks in the backyard. Even if it rained or a gray blanket of fog rolled in from the nearby ocean, I was not allowed back inside until Mother summoned me to clear the table, wash the dinner dishes, clean the cat's litter box with my fingers, and anything else she could conjure. Afterward in the garage and feeling exhausted, I'd do my best to remain perfectly straight, trying not to fall whenever my head fell forward. I'd stay in that position until Mother granted me permission to assemble my army cot bed in the dark. Before drifting off I'd say my prayers, thankful I could escape through my dreams.

I had no television, no neighborhood baseball games, no playing at a friend's house, or even a warm meal. No hugs or sitting on someone's lap, no sharing a laugh, or "that one magical childhood moment" that I would forever cherish. No wonderment or sense of discovery, no self-worth. My home was the darkness of the garage and the disposition I brought with it.

But in some sense living in the garage at least provided a barrier of protection. As I became self-aware, especially after being burned on the gas stove and taking my vow of survival, the garage became a world of its own for me. The garage was far better than shivering outside in the backyard where my hands and shoulders would become numb from sitting on the rocks. And after learning to distinguish the different sounds from above and knowing Mother's television habits, I was able to take down my guard just a notch. Only when I felt it was absolutely safe would I sit down, lower my head, and steal a few minutes of sleep. On some afternoons I was lucky enough to sneak two quick naps before I was required to do the evening chores.

During the summer months I didn't have to worry about the cold, and sometimes I'd smile inside whenever I'd hear the neighborhood kids scream with joy as they rode their bikes down the block. It took me forever to understand that the "clicking" sounds were baseball cards hitting the spokes of their wheels.

I quickly learned that feeling sorry for myself only got me so far, so I vowed to make the most of my time. If I wasn't imagining myself flying away as one of my superheroes, I'd read encyclopedia-sized books that I brought home from school. For years Mother had berated me on how stupid I was, so I tricked her into thinking that I was indeed incompetent and needed to complete extra homework in order to keep up. I knew full well how closely Mother wished to guard our relationship, so our "attention time" became a little shorter than before, as she believed the teachers would question why my homework was not completed. So, between my chores and Mother beating me, I'd strain my eyes in the darkness and race through every page of my books, absorbing every picture in detail and every word of every sentence. Besides school, my favorite part of the day was expanding my imagination by reading books about reptiles or volcanology, or adventure stories like *Robinson Crusoe* or *The Count of Monte Cristo*. Sometimes I would rush through my chores or stand impatiently waiting for Mother to finish doing whatever she did to me, so I could finish another page in one of my books.

On rare occasions, late into the night Mother would turn off the television and play a Bill Cosby record. For me there was no greater treat. Knowing she would soon be going to bed, I felt safe enough to shut my eyes, and while standing I'd imagine Mr. Cosby's words spilling like water. Since Mother played the same record over and over again, I'd study the rhythm of the stories, the timing of the punch lines, how Mr. Cosby spoke with perfect clarity, and his ability to make his characters seem so real. Over time, in my mind I'd lip-sync certain parts of the stories and even though I'd become terrified and stuttered whenever at school or in front of Mother, after hearing Cosby's voice I knew I wanted to become a storyteller. Listening to Bill Cosby was like celebrating Christmas and a birthday rolled into one. Sometimes I'd still shiver in the garage, but whenever I heard, "Hey, Hey, Hey . . . Fat Albert . . ." I'd laugh and all my troubles would melt away.

Being alone gave me the opportunity to educate myself and to plot every move of any situation Mother might dream up. Whenever I felt depressed or self-pity, I'd remember one of Bill Cosby's stories or a passage from one of my adventure books. The darkness became my home. I only had to make it through—one morning, one afternoon, and one evening at a time.

* * *

One winter afternoon I came close to losing it. I hated my life—how unfair everything was and how other people, like my brothers and every kid at school, had more and were treated better than me. That January of 1973 after Father moved out of the house, I felt betrayed. Even though he did little to stop Mother, I always felt safer with his presence upstairs. Somehow I knew with Father gone Mother was going to kill me. The beatings became more intense and far more bizarre. Food became nonexistent.

That Saturday, after not eating for several days, I took the chance of being caught and risked stealing food from the refrigerator just a few feet from me in the garage. I was that desperate: to attempt moving a single inch in the middle of the afternoon—the prime time when Mother might either suddenly open the door to check on me or summon me upstairs to do with me as she pleased. Knowing every inch of the garage and praying my worn-out sneakers didn't make any noise or the hinges to the refrigerator door didn't squeak, I stood on my toes while sliding a frozen pie tin into my hand. I could feel the drool in my mouth while I gazed down at one of Mother's prized homemade pumpkin pies. I knew I could never eat the entire dessert or even take a piece of it. Mother counted every piece of every item of food she kept in the house. Even if eating the pie was my only refuge between life and death, I feared Mother's retributions more. My terror and the rush of cold air escaping from the freezer, coupled with the risk of being caught, made my hands shake so much that I nearly dropped the pie. Caught between survival and fear, I took my chance. With my free hand I pinched a loosened piece of frozen crust, then another and another, until I had a small pile in my hand. Being careful to replace the pie precisely as I had found it, I felt Mother would never know. I had lost track of time, and fearing Mother might get up at any second if a television commercial came on, I scurried back over to my position. Alone in the dark, I blinked my eyes at the prize I cupped in my hand. As my body temperature warmed the frozen crust, I rolled the pieces into a ball. Before popping it into my mouth, I realized how incredibly fortunate I was. Not only did Mother not catch me, but I now held in my hand more food than I had been given in the last few days. I was alive, and I had a keen mind to think with. At least I had a roof over my head, I kept telling myself, and if Mother didn't freak out and kill me, I stood a chance of staying alive. I knew in my heart if I could survive all that I had up till then, anything else had to be a little easier, a little better.

At the bottom of the stairs, the pie crust seemed as if it

was melting in my mouth . . . as if I were eating a grand meal. Even after swallowing I could still taste my bountiful feast. I shivered, but not from the cold, my self-imposed fear, or anxiety. I trembled with the pleasure of fulfillment. I had risked everything to accomplish my task. Alone in the dark I smiled at my good fortune. For a rare moment in my life, I was happy with myself.

* * *

I never forget how lucky I am, no matter what I'm doing in life. When giving a presentation I am almost always asked, "Dave, if you had the chance, what would you change about your past?" And I always give the question serious thought: Would I run away, defend myself from Mother, or maybe have the opportunity to be born to a different set of parents? But for me the answer is always the same: Nothing! I wouldn't change a single element of my former life. As previously stated, and as weird as it may sound, my past experiences—every one of them—as grim and at times terrifying as they were, made me appreciate everything, and I mean *everything*, in my life today. After the experiences I have had, *what* do I really have to complain about?

If there's one thing that drives me crazy it is people who, after living through an unfortunate, extraordinary experience, by their own choice wallow in self-pity or are absolutely miserable for the rest of their lives. Why in the world would someone go through all that pain, suffering, and despair just to be so unhappy? In my case, the first twelve years of my life were not good ones, so I'm going to live the remainder of my sixty to seventy years as best I can.

Why is it a lot of folks are so unhappy? Why are there great numbers of people who, no matter what they have or whatever they strive to achieve, seem so unfulfilled? I'm guessing unresolved issues would play a major role, but part of the solution could be that maybe the older we get, the more complacent, hopeless, and despondent we become. I don't think we mean to; however, some of us may forget that we try to resolve issues, deal with the everyday situations, work hard, sacrifice, and push ourselves for the simple purpose of obtaining some form of satisfaction. And over time we forget what we're fighting for. For one reason or another we believe life burns us out and we forget to *be* happy.

The Race to Grow Up and Get Ahead

Being a film buff, there is one film that I highly recommend, and it's about getting caught up in the daily grind of life: *Hook,* the Steven Spielberg film starring Robin Williams and Dustin Hoffman. The film is an account of what happens to Peter Pan once he's grown up. Mr. Williams plays the role of Peter Banning, who's forgotten he used to be the carefree, adventurous Peter Pan. As an adult, Peter's life consists of high-powered corporate business dealings. In Peter's pursuit of wealth he not only neglects his wife and children, and drinks too much, while griping about every little thing, but he has become the New Age version of a cutthroat pirate. In the course of the film Peter's children are kidnapped by his old nemesis, Captain Hook, and before Peter can rescue his children by doing battle with his adversary, he must relearn what was so critically important to him as a child: the love and security of being part of a family. In other words, Peter Banning must rediscover his happy thoughts. After doing so and defeating Captain Hook in a duel, Peter triumphantly returns home with his children. In the glow of the family reunion Peter is asked, "Are you done with all of your adventures?" Peter, with a childlike grin and a sparkle in his eyes, replies, "To live; now, that would be an adventure!"

Again, it's sad to say, but for so many folks it seems the older they become in the race of "get ahead and have it all," even if they achieve their desires, in the end they lose themselves and that exhilarated innocence. They lose that prime motivating element that made it all possible in the first place. They lose their happy thoughts. When you were younger, what did you aspire to be? What did you wish to do? Are you truly doing what you want today? Overall, are you a fulfilled person?

Naturally, at any given time any of us would answer, "Well, I really don't like what I'm doing now," or "No, at the moment I'm not happy at all." That's the reality of life: we all can't do what we want at every given moment of every day. Now, I'm not saying you should walk through life grinning from ear to ear like your facial muscles are frozen, but I am saying to at least be happy in your quests and the world you live in right now, today. Don't wait to get that job, pass that exam, marry that person, buy that car, or survive some immense crisis for you to be appreciative. Because while you think you are truly happy, you are only basing your happiness on your surroundings or the situation and not yourself as a person. And don't you deserve better than that?

At one time in all of our lives, being happy was the overriding thing on our minds. But, like Peter Banning, as we grew older we lost our happy thoughts. Here's something: From ages two until about fifteen, what do kids think about? Answer: PLAYING! Being happy and exploring everything to its fullest capacity is basically all that's on kids' minds. The younger they are, the more they believe that anything is possible. And they're happy with things that really don't cost a lot or amount to a great deal—holding their hands, reading to them in bed, or giving them praise for something they accomplish. And if they're having a bad day, their world is suddenly brighter when you mention "ice cream." When it comes to gifts, babies and toddlers seem more euphoric over tearing open a box than in discovering what's inside. They spend more time popping the bubble wrap that protected the gift that you broke your back and blitzed through countless malls and waited in line for hours to buy, than they do in playing with it. For some kids, no matter the age, you can't get them to stay in bed even if you put lead weights on them, for the simple reason that they want to play and *play right now*.

Between the ages of fifteen and twenty as they become more mature, these young adults craving independence still wish to play, but do so primarily when adult supervision is nowhere to be found. The older teenagers get, the less they can wait to move out and be on their own, so no one can tell them what to do or how to do it. *Then* life will be grand and they can do whatever they want, at any given moment of any day. Their lives will be completely filled with carefree ecstasy.

Around the ages of twenty to twenty-five, the carefree priorities take a slight shift because of one word from Dr. Abraham Maslow, a gentleman considered the father of modern psychology, who created the pyramid theory of human needs: *Survival*. For the most part, if these twenty-somethings do not have gainful employment, they have difficulty purchasing food and having a place to rest their heads. Amusing themselves and doing all those "adults things" they've dreamt of for so many years is still on their minds, yet college, trade school, and/or landing a job ebbs away at their youthful ambitions.

By the ages of twenty-five to thirty-five, we've pretty much settled into our careers, and saving for our own home and other materialistic things takes precedence. Usually at this age, out of the blue we see that person from across the way, then Cupid shoots his arrow and we fall victim to this crazy emotion called love. We marry, become a little bit pregnant, and soon *the* number-one priority in our lives is to ensure we have an arsenal of Pampers within our reach.

From thirty-five to forty-five, after a few medical examinations, we discover we're not immortal. We can't believe that we not only subjected our bodies to the things we did in our youth—stunts that would surely have gotten us arrested in these days—but that we actually lived to tell about it. We have become our generation's biggest foe: we are now part of the establishment. One day we woke up and became our father, mother, uncle, aunt, or anyone else we despised in our childhood. We join health clubs. We pay exorbitant sums in order to sweat out built-up toxins (in public) and watch, weigh, and worry about every gram of fat that enters our bodies just so we can pay more taxes by living longer. We frantically purchase every piece of workout contraption or video we see on television, and after a few weeks we find ourselves running out of spaces for the "easy-to-use, easy-to-store" revolutionary equipment, so we begin to think about the idea of purchasing a bigger home, just so we can have a bigger garage and more closet space—so we can cram it with more stuff from our lives.

With the greatest of anticipation we try every diet, buy gallons of Rogaine, and in our limited time off we go to the "fake and bake" for that Saint-Tropez tan. Looking young is now the foremost goal in our lives. Stability is important too. The average American has car insurance for her 2.5 cars—that she'll be paying for right up until the warranty expires or the engine blows up in the middle of rush-hour traffic, while she's driving a herd of children in her minivan (that years ago she swore she wouldn't be caught dead in) to soccer practice. We have house insurance, health insurance (including dental), and another policy to take care of whatever the other insurance policies were supposed to. There's insurance for the boat, Wave Rider, and any other toy that makes us happy. After a big scare we purchase tornado, hurricane, flood, earthquake, and "dust bowl" insurance as a package deal—just in case ol' Mother Nature decides to promote chaos. We have insurance protection for not only every credit card we need, but practically every piece of appliance we're still making payments on—the television, DVD player, and Nintendo; the washer, dryer, and refrigerator, to the puree blender that we use for our high-energy, high-carb, high-protein, low-fat, no-taste protein shakes . . . so we can live longer, pay more taxes, and purchase more insurance polices.

We plan ahead, we think about retirement and escaping the rat race once and for all. We invest in the market. We have expanded portfolios that include a carefully analyzed quantity of mutual funds and numerous shares of Starbucks, Worldwide Wrestling Federation Entertainment, and Victoria's Secret. We are waiting for the next Amazon.com or Yahoo.com IPOs, so we can get in, clean up, and dump the stock at a huge profit so Uncle Sam can take his share from our successes. We have heated debates about the virtues and drawbacks of 401Ks and IRAs. We count the days until our lovely children, who were once precious babies but in the last few years have acted as if they've been possessed by demons, move out on their own so we can finally buy that motor home, see the world, and wear pants with the elastic waists.

Around the ages forty-five to fifty-five, for some of us our better days are behind us. We're amazed to find ourselves far more conservative about life in general than we were in our twenties. We find ourselves grumbling more. At the corner café we publicly denounce all politicians as crooks. While reminiscing about the good ol' days of President John F. Kennedy who inspired our nation to journey to the moon and how Richard Nixon made us all eye the office of the president with more suspicion, some *kid* with a double shot of espresso and dash of raspberry syrup looks at you with a who-in-the-hell-are-you-talking-about? expression. At home our relaxation is according to what's scheduled on the television. A bad day for us is not some crisis at work or at the home front, but rather when the television cable craps out or when we temporarily lose the remote control. We "armchair-quarterback" every play of every sport, we screech at our soap-opera stars for sleeping with their best friend's bother's uncle who just woke from a ten-year coma, and we are amazingly surprised at every episode of the *Jerry Springer Show*.

We complain more about how unfair life is to us. We make more excuses of *what could have been*: "If it wasn't for my bad knee from high school, I could have gone on and played pro football." "If I hadn't married you, I could have gone to Hollywood and become a star." We're depressed about the fact that whenever we lose our hair we find it growing in our noses, ears, and other areas that we're too ashamed to discuss in public. But, hey, we tell ourselves, retirement is just around the corner. Then I'll have fun!

From ages fifty-five and beyond, we're just too damn tired to do anything. Late-night television shows like Jay Leno or David Letterman seem so juvenile, and besides it's way past our bedtimes. We complain so much about everything that no one will have anything to do with us, except for those "unknowing hostages" known as *babies*—who, with drool spilling from the side of their mouths, are in giggling awe of the old person sitting in front of them with all that white hair sticking out of both ears.

Since they don't make good shows like they used to, we abandon the television and spend our day spouting wisdom that no one in the world wants to hear: "Back in my day, we didn't have those fancy 'Rybook' or 'Neeke' shoes. And, another thing: we didn't have a school bus or some fancy beau pick us up in their parents' fancy SUV. I tell ya, back in my day we walked three miles to school, up and over the hill, barefoot in the snow every day! And we never complained! Not once, not one iota, not one word! We had it hard and we loved it. Oy, you kids today have it too easy! All you want to do is play, play, play. I tell you what—you better learn to grown up and act your age. Life's not all fun and games. Wait till you're my age, then you'll see. Then you'll know something about something. And another thing—let me tell you about the value of a dollar. Back in my day, that's when a dollar meant something. . . ."

The older generation worries that the younger generation either doesn't work hard enough or doesn't appreciate all of the work and sacrifice of others. The older generation seems to believe that the world *is* going to hell in a handbasket and the *young kids* are the ones wearing the UPS uniforms delivering the goods.

Whatever happened to being happy?

A Cheerful Disposition

In a twisted comical sense, a lot of the above rings true. If we take ourselves too seriously in the pursuit of our endeavors all of our good nature could be used up by the time we achieve what we've wanted. For instance, did you know the average child laughs more than four hundred times a day? For the average adult that number dwindles down to less than forty. So many of us work hard, provide for our families, and sacrifice ourselves to the hilt, so much so that we can easily surrender our inner passions and happiness in the process. All we end up doing is feeding the machine. Get up, to go to work, to pay for the car that gets you to work and provides a means to sustain the home and feed the family, so you can bring home more work, then finally go to bed, only to repeat the process the next day. The hard truth is there are dues to be paid, and efforts and forfeits are facts of life. But as you deal with life's complications and strive to achieve your desires, are you happy? Do you feel proud of yourself or get a tiny rush of excitement that you applied yourself in the right direction? *You should.*

In the midst of applying yourself, dealing with whatever issue life throws your way, are you able to relax? Do you clear your head and take a breather? Or do you find yourself constantly getting wrapped around the axle over the most insignificant petty things that take up a majority of your time, energy, and focus? Are you losing sleep, feeling drained and unsatisfied? Do you find yourself always defending your actions, or does your emotional state seem to be just below the boiling point? The answer could entail an endless number of elements. Again, I'm no psychologist, but I'm guessing that if you answered yes to two or more of these questions you, my dear friend, are not relaxing enough! You need a more cheerful disposition. As we discussed in the first section of this book, you need to empty that CD-ROM in your head. You may need to decompress *from* home *before* you arrive at work or school, *so* you have a clear head and are therefore able to tackle your objectives. Continually take little mental breaks whenever and however you can. *Whatever you do, do something positive.*

By force of habit, whenever I say or think something negative, before it becomes ingrained in my mind, I instantly try to replace it with something positive. While in the vortex of hysteria and confusion I silently tell myself, *Well, it could be worse.* Another line I recommend is from the movie *Point of No Return*: "I never did mind the *little* things." The same attitude is the concept of best-selling author Richard Carlson in his book, *Don't Sweat the Small Stuff . . . and It's All Small Stuff.*

Vent when you need to, but don't allow life's twists and turns and bumps on the road to drain your happiness. The more you take control of your attitude, the more cheerful you will be and the more you'll be able take on and complete any task.

A lot of folks take happiness for granted, as if we as individuals had no say-so over this emotion. But we do. Think about it: all of our lives we've been taught to watch what we say, keep that attitude in check, or don't fly off the handle. By coincidence and through years of conditioning a lot of us neglect to work on a positive attitude. So what do you do? I advise that in all of your efforts as you apply yourself in areas of health, in saving for the future, studying for that test, or in working hard for that new car, each and every day do the same on your positive, upbeat attitude. As always, continue to better yourself but do so *now* by being aware of your emotional state. Replace negative attitudes with positive ones. As you are well aware: as bad as things are, they could be a lot worse. And griping and complaining will not get you out of it, but a simple optimistic attitude can turn things around. Again, in the final analysis it is up to you.

Years ago, before the comedian actress Gilda Radner passed away from her battle with cancer, she formed groups with others who, like her, were fighting the disease, and together they found a sense of happiness and reprieve from their situations. It didn't change the fact that these brave people had to deal with their life-threatening disease every day, but spreading a bit of cheer among themselves made their circumstances the more tolerable. In one interview I heard Ms. Radner say, "I look at it this way: as I'm fighting cancer, I think of all the money I'm saving on shampoo." To this day Gilda's disposition has touched countless others who are surviving cancer with dignity and feeling more fulfilled.

The Power of a Positive State of Mind

Happiness is a state of mind—*your mind*—so you take the control. With everything else you're committing to, in order to better yourself don't take this one vital item for granted. Whenever you step out of a certain comfort zone to enhance the person you wish to be, make sure you have a sense of contentment with each and every step you take. If you're doing all that you can without a sense of joy or even satisfaction, there's a strong chance you may not get to where you want to go. Don't throw this important element into the wind; if you do (and if you have the kind of luck I have) it will end up in the hands of Murphy's Law.

Don't leave your happiness to fate. Even with the best of luck, destiny can only take you so far. Years ago, when I flew in the air force, I had an offbeat friend named George who convinced himself his sole path to happiness was to marry. George never went out. He never mingled. He never dated. Yet every Friday night, he would put on his best imitation polo shirt that he had purchased overseas for five dollars, run a comb through his oily hair, and wait. And wait. And wait. After a year of frustration George expressed his concerns, and although I and others offered suggestions he remained ensconced in his faith for happiness. George believed without a doubt that someday, some woman would show up, knock on his door, and make him a happy man. As romantic as this story may sound, *George* never put forth the effort, any effort, needed to obtain the happiness he believed he so desperately craved.

Why would you waste a day of your life waiting for happiness to find you? Do *something* to manage your own destiny. Don't postpone your elation until after your final exams, completion of that one project, or wait until you take *that* vacation. And don't even think about saying, "I'll be happy *once* I get that car, that promotion, lose that weight, or find that one person I'll spend the rest of my life with." If I may say: Make your own happiness. Be happy with who you are and what you have in your life *right now*!

It wasn't too long ago that I lived in an ice-cold, rundown cabinlike summer home in the middle of winter with no insulation and no heater, sleeping on a leaky air mattress, while literally scraping pennies together. I discovered within hours following my return from Japan after receiving the award and being celebrated as one of the Ten Outstanding Young Persons of the World, that my fortunes had suddenly turned upside down. I had been "mismanaged" by the speaking firm that represented me. After collecting myself, with a strong belief in my own cause, scared to death, and not knowing what lay ahead of me, I decided to start my own business. I paid the price for my ambition, put in twenty-hour days while maintaining a high standard, and even worked a few odds jobs in order to get by. Like anybody else in my position, I took a few hard knocks and there were days that the only meal I could afford was a single serving of Cup-a-Soup. And yet, as hard as it was, as many sacrifices as I made, and at times with so much against me, I loved every minute of it! For me, living in that freezing cabin, in the middle of winter, with wrapping my hands around my soup meal as the only way of warming myself, was one of the greatest, most fulfilling times of my life.

Beyond my health, youth, and a few close friends, I was on the threshold of a new life and I made the most of what I had. I appreciated everything—a place to call my own, the sound of the rain hitting the roof, the smell of the redwood trees after a storm, the hours I spent alone reading a book or listening to music.

Some days I'd splurge by having a piece of three-day-old French bread. With every bite I'd smile, thinking that I had nothing to complain about, for the bread was more than I'd had before. No matter how hectic my day or desperate my situation was, I'd try to find something positive in it. I'd decompress by stepping outside on the wooden deck, sometimes in the chilling rain, looking straight up at the majesty of the trees against the darkened sky. I was optimistic. I was living the American dream, and with every day I was closer to living in a real home, chockful of food and with a fireplace to keep me warm. With hope and opportunity, what more could I *really* ask for?

Maybe it's me, but because of all I endured as a child there is literally not a single day that I wake up and don't appreciate the fact that I am alive, not a day that I'm not optimistic of what is before me. Because of my past I was extremely fortunate to learn as a child how much bitterness my mother held in her heart and how unhappy she was. I vowed not to repeat the mistakes she made—if Mother was so unhappy about her past, I decided to deal with my issues as best as I could, before they would overwhelm me as they had her. Since Mother hated everyone and everything, I've learned, through her destructive lifestyle, to hate no one, especially my own perpetrator. And because I had virtually no life as a kid, I've done my best to ensure that my son can live a life full of wonderment and opportunity, but above all that he will never have to be subjected to what I had to endure as a child. And finally, on a deep personal level, maybe I had to suffer what I did, almost dying several times in the process, in order to cherish the value and sanctity of the life I have today.

Everywhere you go, you take yourself. Never forget: *your* attitude *is* everything. And with all that there is to life, don't leave your happiness to destiny; for your lack of effort and ignorance will only result in a hollow, joyless life.

The primary reason why I'm hammering away at you to be content with who you are and what you have in your life right now is there are no guarantees when you go to sleep at night that you are going to wake up tomorrow morning. None! *This* is why I stressed getting closure on our issues. Don't allow every little thing to get to you, drag you down, and consume your life. There may not be a tomorrow to count on, so live the best life that you can today. As stated in the final scene of the movie *Hook*: "Seize the day!"

No Guarantees for Tomorrow

Years ago I read a poem that to this day has had a profound affect on my life. "If I had my life to live over . . . I'd relax, I would limber up. . . . I would take fewer things seriously. . . . I would climb more mountains and swim more rivers. . . . I would eat more ice cream. . . . I would pick more daisies." This poem was written by Nadine Stair, an eighty-five-year-old woman whose words encouraged many to see and live life through new eyes.

If you had only ten days to live, what would you do? Seriously, if your doctor informed you that you had just a few days to live, what would you do with the time you had left? Now, you might say, "Hell, I'd just see another doctor and get a second opinion." Go ahead; make an appointment, take all the time you need. But your time is slipping away with every wasted hour.

I'd tell you what I'd do: I'd pick up the phone and call anyone that came to mind. I'd make the most of my time and have a blast. I'd surround myself with the sounds of my favorite music and fill every room with the scent and vibrant colors of fresh-cut flowers. I would definitely go on a spending binge. I would surprise family and friends with gifts, in the hopes of showing my appreciation and to make their lives just a little brighter. And even though I'm an introvert, I'd host a few parties so I could hold, hug, and just be with those who were important to me during the course of my life. I'd fight for every minute of my life and try to not to squander my time. I wouldn't sleep, but I'd take naps outside. I would watch every sunrise and every sunset. I would make peace with my God and be appreciative of the time I had on this planet and how fortunate I was.

What does your world of happiness mean to you? What does it truly, absolutely take to make you feel fulfilled? How much does it cost to watch a sunset, to feel the rays of the sun on your face, or to hear the surf crash against a sandy beach? What price can you put on holding the hand of another or the warm embrace of that one person who means the world to you? How much effort does it take to change your pessimistic attitude and do something to brighten someone else's life?

In all my travels I've learned the things that make all of us happy are right in front of us, each and every day. Our happiness is readily available to everyone of us *regardless* of our age, sex, nationality, education, religion, our past, our desires, or how much we have or don't have!

Some time ago I ran into a dear friend who had just returned from vacation. Ray had a perfect tan, a bright smile, and a lively spring in his step. I couldn't stop him from telling me about his recent cruise. "I tell ya, my wife and I, all we did was eat and drink. We spent all day at the pool and danced all night. We watched every sunset. We made love every night. We talked for hours on end, we laughed out loud in front of everybody, and played like kids. I tell ya, that was the best money I ever spent!"

When Ray told me the amount, I nearly swallowed my tongue. "Well," I replied, "you and your wife could have done all that at my house for half the price!"

Of course, I was kidding. Ray is one of the hardest workers I know. He is one of the few people who do for others before thinking of themselves, and that one cruise was a lifetime goal for him and his lovely wife. I just find it odd that some people have to "get away" in order to be happy, or lose—or almost lose—that someone or something that's so special to them in order to truly appreciate what they have in their everyday life; like the saying You don't know what you have till it's gone.

Every Thanksgiving and every holiday season all of us take a moment, bow our heads, and reflect on our blessings. I'm sure nearly all of us, no matter what situation we're currently working on or what we've already been put through, realize how lucky we are. With all the troubles in the world, what if we could carry some of that appreciation and sense of joy with us every day?

Take a step back and look at all that you've accomplished and the opportunities before you. Now ask yourself: What does it take for me to *truly* be happy? The answer has been right in front of you all this time.

HELP YOURSELF REMINDERS

* WE WORK AND SACRIFICE FOR THE CAUSE OF FULFILLMENT.
* A CONSISTENT, POSITIVE ATTITUDE MAKES A WORLD OF DIFFERENCE.
* DON'T LEAVE YOUR HAPPINESS TO FATE.
* THERE ARE NO GUARANTEES FOR TOMORROW, SO APPRECIATE ALL THAT YOU HAVE AND DO ALL THAT YOU CAN TODAY!

7

What Do You Say When You Talk to Yourself?

For once I was actually happy to run home. Since my parents' separation just a few weeks ago, I finally had something to smile about. After years of trying to prove to Mother that I wasn't stupid or worthless, I clinched my verification in the palm of my hand.

Just days before the school's winter break, my homeroom teacher, Mr. Ziegler, had come up with an idea of having the students name the school paper. Everyone entered and I, too, came up with a catchy phrase. I never gave it much thought partly because I knew if the kids found out that "Pelzer-Smelzer" had reached the finals, they would all vote against me. But as the numbers to the selections were broadcast over the loudspeaker, my phrase had captured nearly every vote. Before dismissing the class for the weekend, Mr. Ziegler announced to the students that the idea was mine, and to my surprise everyone clapped and howled with applause. I swelled with pride. As my teacher gave me an envelope to present to Mother, he assured me that Mother, too, would be proud.

Before closing the front door to Mother's house, I gazed up at the gray clouds beginning to take form. Seconds later, I stood in front of Mother with my chin to my chest, but this time I extended my arm, revealing the crumpled envelope I held out for her.

After Mother leaned from the couch to snatch the letter, I stole a quick glance. As she tore open the envelope and her eyes swept through Mr. Ziegler's writing, my pulse raced with anticipation. I swallowed hard, waiting for her reaction. I kept thinking, *This is it. Someone has publicly stated that I, David Pelzer, am okay.* For years Mother had fought to justify her "treatment" of me because I was either troubled, pathetic, or simply a slow child. But now, I thought to myself, for someone to write a letter by hand, signing his name to it—it is now official! Mother couldn't brush it off as she always did when I brought home good grades on my report card, claiming I had somehow changed the D's to B's. That I couldn't be that bright. That I had somehow cheated. Now, in Mother's hands, was the confirmation I had wished for for years: *I am a good kid.*

"Well," Mother huffed after pausing to wipe the side of her face, "it says here, your teacher claims you were the student to name the school paper." She stopped for a moment, nodding her head ever so slightly as if taking everything in. "Aren't you the special one?"

I stood in front of Mother almost revealing my grin

as she again read through the letter. Without thinking I raised my head to look up at Mother, searching for the smallest reaction. In a sudden flash Mother erupted, with her pointed finger almost striking my face. "Get one thing straight. There is nothing, nothing, you can do to impress me, not now, not ever! Do you understand? You are nothing to me. Nothing, a nobody, an 'It.' You don't even exist. I hate you and wish you were dead. Do you hear me? Dead!"

I was too numb to say anything as Mother stood up and ripped Mr. Ziegler's letter into pieces. All I could do was stare up as the letter that I had placed all of my hope upon rained down on me like snowflakes from a winter storm. Kneeling to the floor, I tried to somehow put the letter together. I thought if I did, then maybe something would turn out, as if that one piece of paper would help me through all of my problems. But I couldn't fix it. There were too many pieces, and in my heart I held the truth I had always known. So I, too, repeated Mother's words: that I did not exist and wished I was dead.

With Mother standing in her slippers just inches in front of me, I scooped the flakes of my prized paper before dumping them into the kitchen trash can. After completing my series of afternoon chores, I stood perfectly still in the garage. I stared straight ahead at the worn red-colored stairs with the black matting that Mother herself had painted and tacked on years ago. While on the outside I seemed almost robotic, on the inside I had completely lost it. During all the years and thousands of times Mother went out of her way to call me names or put me down, I had somehow brushed everything off. I had always believed, I had always felt from the recesses of my soul, that it was the booze talking or something else that took over Mother that made her treat me as she did. In my years of desperation, every day I had anticipated that tomorrow might be the day—the one day that she would wake up from her stupor and we would reunite as a normal mother and son. But while staring into my world that darkened as the night began to fall, there was no escaping my reality. I knew by the tone of her voice, by the cold, sickening gleam of pure pleasure pouring from her eyes, that Mother had meant every syllable. *I was a nobody.* A nonexistent thing. To Mother I would always be known as the child called "It."

* * *

To this day I can still hear Mother's words ringing in my ears and, at times, in my heart. But I am no different from anyone else. All of us have heard such words, if not worse ones, during the course of our lives. It has been said by many in the field of psychology that as individuals it's not the physical pain that we carry with us, but the psychological trauma that hurts us the most. I'm sure you, too, can remember not only what that particular person said to you, but also the look on his face, the time of day, and what was going on in the background. When I work with those who still seem affected by such an event, I recommend for them to look at where that finger of defeat is connected. The individual saying those things or jabbing that finger in your face is not a happy person. In my mother's case she was, for whatever reason, miserable with herself, and she simply took it out on me. She projected her frustration, guilt, shame, and everything else she kept bottled up inside over the years, onto her husband, children, her mother, other family members, and anyone else until her animosity spread to everyone and anything she came in contact with.

This is why it is so critical to address and resolve your issues. No one's perfect, all of us have said and done things we regret. And if you have said some hurtful things, as I've already recommended make amends as best as you can. That doesn't mean you surrender or that you were wrong. But if you still carry some psychological scar, imagine how others, especially those close to you, feel when they hear such words.

Even though what we hear can have a tremendous impact on our lives, that doesn't mean we're doomed. Every day all of us are subjected to tremendous amounts of negativity ranging from home, work, our community, portions of the news, and especially from those we're close to. We are bombarded by so much negativity that part of us may become immune. It's hard to process it all, let alone remain optimistic. If you feel frayed at times, trust me, it's normal. Did you know that the average person from the moment she wakes up to the time she goes to sleep and loses consciousness, has between forty thousand and fifty thousand thoughts a day? That's on the average. Imagine how many thoughts Albert Einstein or

Carl Sagan had, or Stephen Hawking contemplates. Now, if a person is awake eighteen hours a day, that's over twenty-two hundred thoughts an hour, which equates to over thirty-six separate thoughts a minute; which means every other second, you and I have a single concept racing through our heads. And that's every other second of every day for the rest of our lives. No wonder we're so frustrated and tired!

Now, take into account that the average person who, again, has at least forty thousand thoughts every day swimming around in her head, spends nearly ninety percent of her energy talking to herself. Ninety percent! We see folks we don't know, size them up, and decide within seconds whether we like them or not. Without warning we find ourselves in a situation and rather than hear what's being said about the matter at hand, our brains scream "Oh, my God!" Or at a social occasion, when three or more people are gathered around you it always seems that there's one idiot who drones on, and on, and on. Inside you're itching to jump in. You're looking for a pause, as if you're in a "tag team" wrestling match waiting for your turn . . . then *you'll* be able to get in your two cents, so *you* can spout your ideas and impress others, while someone beside you is looking for a sign of momentary lull so he, too, can pounce on the conversation.

And as if all of this weren't confusing enough, out of those forty thousand thoughts, in which ninety percent of your time is spent talking to yourself, at least seventy-five percent are *negative*. With everything we hear from others about ourselves, whatever news we see or hear, or no matter what's going on in our lives, no one, and I mean no one, can put us down as we ourselves can: *I'm not good enough, smart enough, or pretty enough. I'm too fat, too thin, too old, or not old enough. No one likes me. I'm not worthy. I hate myself. I wish I were dead.*

At one time or another *all* of us have had dejected thoughts. Hopefully they have been fleeting ones. None of us lives in a "happy land" animated world filled with lollipops and ginger snaps. In the course of my life I've learned this: Every single one of us is worthy. All of us have unique gifts that no one else can duplicate. Bad things happen to us and against us. How can you accomplish your objective if you don't believe, and I do mean *truly believe* in yourself first and foremost? So, if you find yourself being constantly dominated by unhappy thoughts about yourself, I highly advise you to seek and receive professional guidance and support. Don't waste another moment of your precious life. Better yourself, by getting some help for yourself.

I'm sure no one grows up with the intention of being exposed to so much negativity or having all these pessimistic thoughts running around in her head. But in an awkward sense, negativity has been enforced into all of our lives. Think about it this way: What is the first word from a baby's mouth? Now, some might say *Mama* or maybe *Dada*. There are some adults, particularly grandparents, who boast that their four-month-old prodigy has articulated *Gaga*. Yet, for the most part, the first words from the mouths of babies is *NO*.

As babies begin to discover their world, they are into

everything all at once, all the time. When my son was a toddler, whenever he was put in his little walker he was, for lack of better words, hell on wheels. There was no way I could keep up with him; but I stupidly attempted to do just that. I found myself sprinting after him fast and furiously for the sole purpose of assuring his safety. Whenever Stephen would make a sudden turn around a corner, I'd run after him at warp speed keeping my eyes right on him, fearing what he might get into, and I would literally smash headfirst into the wall at the end of the hallway. I soon found myself barking, "No, no, no"—a hundred, thousand, million, billion times a day. "Stephen! Don't go so fast! Don't pry off the cover and stick your finger in the electrical socket! Don't eat that plant! No, the kitty's tail doesn't come off! And, no, Stephen, do not lift up your aunt's skirt and use it as a tent in front of company. No, no, no!"

During childhood all of us are bombarded with reasonable, protective instructions like: *Don't take candy from strangers; Make sure you look both ways before you cross the street; Never get into a car with someone you don't know;* to the bizarre directives like: *Now, make sure you always wear clean socks and underwear, just in case you get into a car accident, then you won't embarrass yourself with holes in your socks or soiled underpants.* As kids grow older, adults are tired of explaining why, so they simply badger commands: *Wet paint. Don't touch. Off limits. Stay out. You're too young to watch that. Don't say that. You can't listen to* that *kind of music. Don't you even think about* that! *Just say no to drugs. You're not wearing that thing in public!* No, No, No, No!

Now, don't get me wrong. I'm a firm believer in boundaries. But what began as genuine concern for our safety and well-being from those who cared for us, without conscious intent became infused by negativity.

Initial Input

So, is there anything we can do about it? Yes: *Watch what you say when you talk to yourself.* Now, while some folks claim that whatever thoughts run through their heads or whatever words fly out of their mouths about any given situation are not a problem for them, with all due respect I beg to differ. Some time ago I asked seven people—of both sexes and of different ages and levels of education, and various backgrounds—to be a part of a onetime experiment. From the moment they opened their eyes when they woke up, all they had to do was record the first five to ten minutes of their day. Every one of them had the same basic reaction: they got out of bed, gazed at the bedroom clock feeling okay, continued to wake up as they wobbled their way to the bathroom, did their business, washed up, and felt relieved without a care in the world . . . right up until they saw themselves in the mirror. That quickly, in the blink of an eye, they either felt apprehension, a sense of numbness, or were in complete shock. The responses were: *Crap, it's Monday!; I better get the kids up and ready for school; I gotta clean the house and go to the grocery store; I knew I should have studied for that test; I hate going to work and fighting that traffic; I hate my hair; I'm so fat; Oh, my God . . . I'm going to be late!*

Every one of these folks was perfectly fine, completely content with their lives the first two minutes or so of their new day, until they told themselves *how* to react. In every case, they didn't have a care in the world for the simple reason that *they did not have a care in the world*. But as they woke up, the more that CD-ROM in their brain spun to life, a random thought or two triggered an emotional response forcing these folks to react a certain way. Does this sound familiar? Have you ever had the same experience? I have. For me, everything's fine and dandy for the first couple of minutes, then one thought instantly connects with another, which can send my heart racing with all the things I have to accomplish on that given day or that one unresolved problem that's been weighing on my mind. At times in the past, I've allowed myself to get so wrapped up in a small band of negative thoughts that has had an adverse effect on my day, *until* I either replaced the negative perceptions with something positive or simply dealt with whatever the issue was and let it go.

Did you know when you conceive just one solitary thought, that message, with the speed of light, sends out thousands of impulses throughout your entire body telling it how to react? Before you can snap your fingers, your body has complied with whatever command initiated from the supercomputer chip within your head. *Wham!* It's that fast. You see that person from across the room and *wham*: you know you don't like him. You catch a whiff of that appetizer you are allergic to and *bing*: you're going to be sick. The pulsating sound of that music is going to give you a splitting headache. You cringe because that person has the coldest hands. Of all the things we taste, touch, see, smell, and hear, our responses are directly related to our initial, internal conceptions.

Have you ever said out loud or to yourself, "I don't feel so good"? Then slowly but surely your senses seem to amplify themselves, reinforcing that one single idea until soon enough you're sick as a dog.

Another example of negative reinforcement is, what do most of us think about after three o'clock on Sunday afternoon? *Arrgghh! Tomorrow's Monday! I gotta go to work. I gotta do all that crap. I'm gonna be buried underneath paperwork or in endless stupid meetings. Man, where did the weekend go?* There are still hours left in our afternoon and we have the entire evening at our disposal but, for most of us, once we see that clock read after four in the afternoon, our minds are a million miles away. The same can be said for those in their last days of vacation time. Even though folks are a thousand miles away from the daily grind, they've allowed their negative thoughts to *ruin* the time they have left.

Positive Input

On the other side of the coin, what do most of us think about on *Thursday* afternoon after three o'clock? "Oh, yeah, Friday! Can't wait. One more day and I'm outta here!" Whether it's work, school, or just getting away from it all for a while, you're completely jazzed because you've just told yourself what's around the corner. The funny thing is, when Friday rolls around you *still* have the same amount of work, still have to go to school to take that test, or get the house together, or do all the things that you detested not even a day ago, but *now* you don't mind. *The only thing different is what you said to yourself.* It's that plain and that simple! Again, your attitude *is* everything!

All you need to do is reprogram what you say when you talk to yourself. It may not be easy, and like anything in life, it didn't happen overnight, so don't expect it to go away overnight. And as we discussed before, when you want something bad enough, there's a price you pay. In this case, readjusting your attitude and how you talk to yourself and perceive all that's thrown at you will take a fair amount of focus and practice on your part. But if you don't at least try to get a handle on what you think and say, even with the best of intentions and all the drive in the world, with all due respect, you, my friend, will only go so far. I believe that a headful of negative thoughts is like swimming across the English Channel, against the tide, and with lead weights. How can you reach your greatness, your true potential, if you don't have yourself in your own corner? Now, I'm not saying for your ego to grow so huge that your head can't pass through a doorway; No! At least, at the very least, believe in yourself and give yourself the respect and dignity that *you* deserve.

So, you want a change in attitude? Let me give you

two words: THINK DIFFERENTLY! From now on, when Monday morning arrives, since there's nothing you can do to change your external environment, since you can't change the calendar, say to yourself, "Once I knock out this day, I only have three more days until Friday!" "Yeah, today may be a long one, but I get a break in another hour." "Just five more years and these kids will be out of my hair!" With everything you attempt, with everything you tackle—whether it's studying for a test, working on your body, or trying to relax when those dreaded relatives from another planet drop by for a month's long stay—it is vital for you to maintain an overall positive attitude.

For the sake of this example, let's say I'm a doctor and I have twin patients that I have just examined and I say, "Ladies, I am sorry to tell you this, but . . . both of you have a strange genetic illness."

Immediately one of the twins leaps out of her chair, screaming at the top of her lungs before fleeing the office, and runs into the street and gets hit by a bus.

The other twin takes a deep breath as she dabs away a tear before asking, "How bad is it, Doc?"

"Well, it's not that bad at all. The illness you have is benign. I can give you a local and you'll be back on your feet in no time. By the way, where is that sister of yours?"

If you tell yourself that your world is going to end, guess what—and don't be surprised: sooner or later it will. If you tell yourself you're not worthy or you cannot accomplish something, your body will respond to the brain's command.

I am telling you that you are worthy, that you have a sense of purpose and belonging. If you didn't, you would never have picked up this book, read as much as you have, and still wanted more. As always, it's up to you. Outside influences can only help you so far. And, as always, you have to not only want it, but you have to be willing to pay the price, and maintaining a confident mind-set is part of your dues. Trust me: little by little, hour by hour, it will pay off. Sometimes the smallest things can make a world of difference. Years ago, I read a magazine article based on two extremely competitive athletes. After lifting weights for hours, one athlete turns to the other and mocks, "Hey, let's see if you can squat five hundred pounds."

The other, who's just a tad bit shorter, eyes the bar with the stack of weights on it and shakes his head, "Nope, can't be done."

"Come on," mocks the taller one, "give it a try!"

The other athlete shakes his head before muttering, "All right, I'll give it a try, but I know I can't do it." To no one's surprise the man levels the bar with the enormous weights on his shoulders, bends slightly to squat the weight, but quickly rises before he reaches the appropriate level of the exercise. After replacing the bar on the rack, the man shakes his head, panting to his antagonistic friend, "See, I told you I couldn't do it!"

The other man rubs his chin. "I bet you one hundred dollars, cash money, right now, that you can squat that weight."

Suddenly the tired athlete's eyes light up. The entire

look on his face changes. And, as you can probably guess, the weary athlete takes a few deep breaths, channeling his attention solely on the bar before he lifts the weight and executes a perfect squat.

So, what was difference between his first, futile attempt and his triumphant second one? After his failure the odds were overwhelmingly against him. He had expended all his energy with his first try, making it almost impossible for him to accomplish a second effort. And, during all this time, the muscles around his legs were beginning to tighten. To top it all off, he had already spent hours working out different muscle groups throughout his body.

The only thing that changed was this professional's attitude. His mind transformed his entire being and became motivated to win the monetary prize. He shifted his inner focus from what he couldn't do, to what he must and would do, in order to obtain that one singular goal.

Maybe you don't know—or maybe you forgot—but you, too, have accomplished the same thing. Okay, maybe you haven't squatted five hundred pounds, but you've overcome something in your life that was far more vital than forming your quadriceps. Maybe you became mad. Maybe you were scared, or tired of hearing or experiencing the same ol' thing. Whatever the circumstance, in the blink of an eye you changed *how* you thought about something and because of that *you changed your outcome.*

The *F* Word

If you look at our country's history, it was founded upon these two words: *optimistic determination*. Imagine, if you will, the thoughts of those who suddenly found themselves on Plymouth Rock. What about those who trekked across the vast open plains? Or the impression of those who awoke one Sunday morning and found themselves in the middle of a world war? As an individual, you could say, "Well, I don't know; we may sink if we sail across that there ocean." Or "Maybe it's best to stay where we are; why would we wanna go that far west anyway?" Or "Well, heck. We're licked. They got the jump on us. What's the use anyhow?" If you or someone you know has that defeatist attitude, he might as well screech in public, run around like a madman, only to get hit by a bus, just because someone uttered something he didn't want to hear.

As parents, what is the primary reason to have kids engage in sports? So they can learn a sense of fair play and to have them discover for themselves what they're made of.

When Stephen first joined the swim team, to be honest he had no right being in the pool. He could barely keep his head above water and as much as he tried, whenever he became tired I believe Stephen expected to have someone jump in at the last second and take care of him. During one of his first swim meets, Stephen gave it his best, but, alas, could not swim the laps required, so he hung on to the flotation dividers, panting, with all of his energy spent, until he realized no one could or would jump in to help him. So one day, out in the middle of a swimming pool, my son, like millions of other children, when faced with a situation he couldn't deny, kept his cool, and drove away whatever defeating thoughts permeated his mind, so he could extend one stroke, then another, then another, until he reached his goal. As a parent, what mattered most to me was that Stephen kept his head above water and didn't quit.

The *only* way to keep your head above water is to convince yourself *you are* going to make it. There's no other way around it. That's life. At times you will find yourself out in the middle of nowhere, bobbing, all alone, surrounded by an overwhelming vastness, with no one to throw you a life ring, while fighting a wall of water that keeps hitting you and hitting you, wave after wave after wave. It can only take a tablespoon of water to do you in. So, what keeps you afloat? What keeps you going? It's whatever you have stored in your noggin. This is what separates those who succeed from those who sit on the sidelines. Not only do you have to want it more, you have to know in your head and in your heart, without a shred of doubt, that you will—not can, but will—accomplish your task.

The key word is *focus*. When you channel your energies on what you can accomplish it replaces your self-inflicted apprehension. You simply replace your negativity, your fear, your whatever, with something indisputable. Forward or reverse. Sink or swim. In the end, as always, it's up to you.

Take baseball legend Mark McGwire: his focus is so intense during a game that he does not make eye contact with anyone or anything that might break his concentration. The day Mark smashed the all-time seasonal home run record, during the postgame interview he stated, "I believe I can accomplish anything I set my mind to. I've said for the last four or five years that the mind's the strongest thing on your body. It will overtake anything you want to overtake."

Focus.

Focus is my *F* word. I'm not trying to sound racy, but I believe every one of us should think about this *F* word and act on it—every hour of every day of our lives. Focus, focus, focus. In everything you do and say, ask yourself the three important questions, just as motivational personality Roger Crawford teaches. And he is a person who truly knows the powerful influence of what you say when you talk to yourself. *Where* are you at? *What* are you doing? And *Where* are you going? As simplistic as these questions sound, they have resonated within me since I was a child.

Back then, not a single day or even an hour slipped by that I did not evaluate my circumstances and harness whatever I could to better myself. When I say to you, *sometimes the smallest things can make a world of difference,* I swear to you that I truly do mean it. It was not just being aware of my dire situation that enabled me to survive, but more so my centralized concentration. It got me through the torrid hell that my mother subjected me to, propelled me through foster care, allowed me to enlist in the air force and become an aircrew member, and enabled me, against a fair number of obstacles, to have a capable career as an author and presenter. But what matters most, what carries me through the seemingly tumultuous times, is what I was able to acquire, learn, build upon, and harness over the course of many years: a quiet sense of inner determination.

Because of my unfortunate past, I value not what hangs on my wall, the accolades I have displayed in the hallway, the car I drive, whatever clothes hang in the closet, or the arsenal of food in my cupboards. But I value that one thing, that constant drive playing in the back of my head that keeps me on track, ensuring that I will *not* repeat a senseless tragedy of living the rest of my days full of hate and destructiveness. That at any given time, any given situation, I can tap into my secret weapon enabling me to become a fulfilled person and a loving husband. As a parent my sole focus has been and will continue to be ensuring that whatever ill I had experienced will not be passed on to my son.

Focus, focus, focus. Ask yourself, where are you at, right now in your life? What are you truly doing to better yourself or your situation? And where on earth are you going? If you lack a central bearing in your life, replace your doubts, your fears, your whatever, with a positive sense of direction. As in the previous section, be consistent every day, but do so now by fixating on the positive.

When I give credit to Mr. Crawford for his positive self-attitude, I do so with the utmost respect. Roger was born without hands or one leg, and he could easily have obsessed on life's unfairness or on the amount of hardship in his everyday life. Instead, with the aid of prosthetics for his leg and after receiving surgery on his left hand, and a lot of personal determination, Mr. Crawford not only played football in high school, but became the first physically handicapped tennis player to be certified as a teaching professional by the United States Professional Tennis Association. As a teenager he became so secure in himself, as one of his high-school coaches told me, that he showed up for a match with his foot deliberately turned backward. To this day Mr. Crawford is happily married, a father, and inspires others to look past their self-induced limitations.

Brad Van Liew, who sailed around the world alone—a voyage that took him over twenty-seven thousand miles—claims being focused literally kept him alive. "There's no question that the 'Around Alone' is a mental as well as a physical battle. If you're going to handle it, you've got to be tough when it counts." During the course of Brad's grueling nine-month adventure, he dealt with loneliness, sleep deprivation that allowed him a mere three hours of rest a night, and physical endurance in which he had to change the ship's sails thirty to forty times a day. Then, of course, there was Mother Nature. Mr. Van Liew fought to keep his fifty-foot ship afloat amid the thirty-foot waves that capsized his fellow competitors, and another storm that nearly put Brad out of the race by destroying his seventy-five-foot mast. In the end, pitted against tremendous odds and the world's greatest sailors, Mr. Van Liew finished third. So how did he do it? In his own words, Brad states, "You can fulfill your own dreams if you really want to. If there's something you really want to do, something you want to remember on your deathbed, make sure you do it. First, make a plan: start with small steps and work your way up to it. You can set out to do the hugest task in the world, but what you need to focus on is the next little task on your way to reaching it. That way it isn't overwhelming."

Final words of encouragement from Brad conclude with, "People who want to push themselves, to discover what they're capable of physically and mentally, will probably discover that it's easier than they think. It *is* hard to tell yourself to do something that doesn't make sense in your head, like sailing alone around the world. But it certainly isn't impossible."

In the final analysis Mr. Van Liew's positive attitude in the middle of nowhere pulled him through, after fighting to remain afloat during those storms, and then on the last leg of his journey when he lost his carbon fiber mast.

Imagine the endless heated debates inspired by the mere *idea* of sailing a ship beyond the *edge of the world.* "Why, that's blasphemous! Everyone knows the world's flat!" The same can be said of fighting the spread of infection before the advent of penicillin. Or the outlandish boldness of having mankind walk on the moon. "No way, absolutely not. It's just way beyond our reach." A lot of nos, a lot of negativity in the air, but the tide turned when that one person said to himself, "But what if . . . ?"

Turning Adversity to Your Advantage

Yet there are times and situations when even the word *no* itself isn't all that detrimental. As I've stated before, because of my past I was fortunate enough to make something positive from it. Just as did John Walsh from *America's Most Wanted,* Gilda Radner for those fighting cancer, and Marc Klaas, the father of the late Polly Klaas and president of the Polly Klaas Foundation. In most matters it takes an unpleasant or even a critical situation to cause something good.

Personally, in some instances I like the word *no.* If there's something I'm set on, or something I may have taken for granted, and now suddenly there's an obstacle in my path, it makes me all the more focused. I become more dedicated if I truly believe in what I'm attempting. Especially when it comes to others who may deliberately go out of their way to obstruct my goals, I think, I pray, I constantly reevaluate my position and dedication. Throughout the process I try to remain calm and not take things so personally. If I do, it takes away from my *F* word: my focus. And I don't push myself and fight as hard as I do for the purposes of revenge or to put others down. I do so for me; to discover for myself if whatever I'm striving for is what I really desire. But I mainly exert myself to see what I'm made of. I never mind paying the price. At times, in the middle of my crusade, when the odds are against me, I go into overdrive. In the end, no matter the results, I'm more appreciative. I can be proud that I at least gave it my all. When I see that "finger of defeat" pointed in my direction, I take a breath and from deep within my heart, I smile.

Sometimes negative words or situations can literally force us to "step up to the plate." All of us have had to cram for that test, muster up more strength during a sporting event, or work smarter at the workplace. And as you well know, our results were far better than we expected. Years ago a friend of mine, Tina, was in the middle of an emotionally trying divorce and had committed herself to losing some weight—against her former husband's expectations. She informed me that during their relationship, Tina's husband constantly berated her about her size. In the beginning my friend wanted to lose weight, mainly out of spite. Tina's goal was to step into their favorite restaurant, wearing a black spaghetti-strap dress, with all eyes—especially her ex's—on her. As motivation can be a valuable tool, Tina was able to *rid* herself of the weight quicker, when I convinced her to do it for herself and not just for revenge.

And, yes, Tina waltzed into the restaurant. And, yes, all eyes were on her. Her former husband's mouth had to be scraped up from the floor, and everyone was astounded when Tina, who once had been shy and soft-spoken, now waved her freshly manicured red fingernail at this man and uttered, "Big mistake! Huge!"

Another friend of mine, Helen, one of my former air force superiors, told me about how she turned things around for herself. "In my day, because I was a girl I always heard no. Girls don't play sports. Women can't have a professional career. And it's not like the air force exactly welcomed me with open arms. I always had to work harder and faster just to make par with my male counterparts. But inside I knew. I knew my capabilities and my self-worth." Helen not only obtained one of the highest ranks in the air force, but also became the squadron's first sergeant in charge of the 350-plus personnel. When not on call twenty-four hours a day, the person who couldn't achieve because of her gender not only had a stellar career, but raised two teenage girls, completely on her own while pursuing a master's degree.

I asked Helen how she felt after having swum against the tide for so many years. "Wouldn't change a thing. I earned it. Respect, dignity, you name it. I earned it all. I held my head high and pressed on!" "And what about all those folks who put you down?" I asked her. "I never did mind much. I got used to it. I turned it around to my advantage. Folks who put you down aren't willing to work as hard. They're so busy discouraging everyone else, they lose their edge. All I did was say to myself, 'Watch out, don't count me out.' " Smiling at me, Helen concluded, "If I teach my girls anything, it's they're going to be exposed to a lot of negativity and no one can change that. It's how they discern and process that information that counts. It's all in the head. Mind over matter. *I don't mind and the trivial rubbish doesn't matter.*"

On the extreme side of the scale, when it comes to telling someone what he can't do, is one of the country's greatest track stars, Steve Prefontaine. Just hours before an important track meet, Steve severely injured his foot. Now, imagine the excruciating pain of setting a record, running for miles with a swollen foot with stitches between your toes. "Doc said no, coach said don't do it. But being stupid and getting my foot mangled brought me back to reality and made me want it more."

Do you remember the 1984 Summer Olympics when Greg Louganis struck the edge of the diving board with his head? Imagine the force of all that weight coupled with the momentum. Imagine slicing your head in front of millions of people watching you from all over the world. Yet this professional had the inner determination to climb back up the ladder, stand on the edge of the diving board, spring up, and execute a perfect dive, capturing the gold medal. When asked how did he make such an incredible comeback, Mr. Louganis basically stated, "I was definitely scared. I had a fair amount of doubt. I just pushed it away. I worked hard my entire life for this one moment. I couldn't just walk away."

As a teenager, when Michael Jordan was told he was not *good enough* to make the cut for his high-school basketball team, I can only guess how determined that made Michael, forcing him to practice far more than his peers, and with far more intense enthusiasm.

Oprah Winfrey, Arnold Schwarzenegger, Nelson Mandela, Gilda Radner, Michael Jordan, Colin Powell, along with countless others brushed aside whatever negativity faced them and instead decided for themselves, focusing on something better. You and I are no different.

What You Make of Your Internal World

None of us can escape negativity; it's only how we deal with it that truly matters. When it comes to maintaining an optimistic attitude, there is no way in the world that any of us can or ever will evade the word *no* or the traces it has on us all. In fact, you will be subjected to million upon millions of *no*s, along with a host of other skeptical words and phrases. But it takes only one single *yes* to turn things around. And that solitary word has to first resonate from within you.

When it comes to no and all of its connotations, plain and simple: we are immersed in it. Given that fact, the only option we have is to learn to adapt. As I said before, I don't mind the word no. Besides my upbringing and all the negativity that went with it, I have had so many people in my life who have gone out of their way to put me down, trip me up, or make me feel as if I were completely moronic or not worthy enough. I've also known some who have worked themselves into a vicious frenzy to ensure they either kept me in my place or would never allow me to reach my goal. And many of you have had your own negative experiences with others. Again that's a fact of life. Nothing's free. And if everything in life were that easy, everyone would be doing it.

Because of my former situation, I was able to learn how extremely vital it was to influence and control whatever I said to myself. Once, during one of my afternoon kitchen beatings, I found myself unable to crawl away. I simply lay sprawled out on the floor with blood pouring from my mouth and nose. Between kicks, Mother would rant the same words that I had heard all of my life. And yet through the pain and even a sense of numbness, I remember turning my head, making eye contact with Mother, and, out of nowhere I smiled at her. I pierced deep into her eyes and vowed to myself, *I'm going to make it. You'll see, one day I'm going to make it. You're not going to break me. I'm better than that.*

At that time I didn't feel vengefulness against Mother or pity for myself, but rather a secure sense of pride and self-worth. I knew on the outside that Mother thought I was stupid. To her I was worthless, weak, only useful as a thing to vent her problems on. I stuttered; I smelled. In a word: I was pathetic. But I heard a tiny, quiet voice within me that persisted in the midst of the madness saying I would somehow, someday, become the person on the outside that I was from within.

It worked. Once I was rescued and placed in foster care, and as teenager desperately trying to be normal and fit in—so someone might, maybe, just maybe, like me—I quickly saw how many teens *acted* and how fast they got themselves in extreme detrimental situations. Yes, I was a geek, nerd, wacko, weirdo, ash-white, pimple-faced, skinny rat with glasses . . . on the outside. But I kept telling myself every single day and sometimes many times during the day, if needed, "I didn't survive all that crap just to throw everything away." Even though I wasn't cool, didn't have a girlfriend or drive a car, or even have the latest shoes, I knew I was okay. In the end, when it mattered most, I would stand on top of any mountain that I chose.

If I may, for my young adults reading this now—and this is after seeing and experiencing all that I have and working with young adults as long as my son's been alive—my advice to you is: Stick to your guns. Don't throw your best away. *You are better than that.* With all the frustration and immense temptation out there, not now but one day soon *you will* have the things you want and be able *to do as you please*. And when you do, I guarantee you that you'll appreciate the life *you made for yourself* all the more. Why? Because you did it. You held your head high. You showed some resolve, some discipline, and didn't plunge after every quick fix that came your way. Now, my dear friend, that is the makings of a mature person, or in other words: a responsible adult.

On every major thing I've attempted, I've always had to crawl my way to success. As a foster kid in a new neighborhood, there was one lady who exclaimed, "Oh, my Gawd! You're one of those—those *foster children*! I don't know what you did to become what you are, but let me give you a piece of advice: Stick to your own kind. If you try to make it, you'll only end up disappointing yourself. But I can see that you're quite used to that, aren't you?" Even though I felt like a worthless tiny ant in front of her, I kept my cool, clutching my hands behind me while smiling back.

When the air force said they didn't want me, I smiled inside, developed a plan, and showed up every day for over six months at the recruiter's office until I wore them down. It took me another three years and endless hurdles and disappointments until I received one yes to have the chance of becoming an aircrew member. I have had obese, disheveled, clip-on-suspenders types of "professional motivational speakers" dribble to me that I wasn't "cookie cutter" enough, and because I was *abused* that I didn't stand a chance of possibly inspiring others. I won't even begin to go into my journey of becoming a bona fide author and eventually working with a New York–based publisher—finally having professionals on my side. For years upon years I've stood up to my ears in insults and negativity. Yet because of what I learned that one day sprawled out on the kitchen floor, I've remained focused on my prize, made an effort every day to improve my position, and kept a clear head while all the time smiling inside, saying, "Don't count me out. I've fought hard before and will do so again. In the end, righteousness will prevail."

You are no different. You've fought battles and you've overcome struggles; so tell me, tell yourself: what got you through it all? What was the one thing that carried you over the hump? That made you take all those hits and remain standing tall? YOUR INNER ATTITUDE. It was *what you said to yourself* when push came to shove. At that one fraction of that one second, out of those fifty thousand thoughts you had swimming around in your head, you said, "Thanks, but no thanks. I'd like to, but I have other obligations. I'm better than that. I'm not much now, but watch out: I'll be back! I am somebody and I'm worth it!" "Sail across the world, you're right: that's never been done before . . . but what if . . . ?" *People who want to push themselves, to discover what they're capable of physically and mentally, will probably discover that it's easier than they think. . . . It certainly isn't impossible.*

One, just one, positive thought can change your attitude, tell your body how to react, can lead you to that one tiny action that can change the course of your life and the world around you; can help you fulfill not only your dreams but your destiny. Just one thought!

You need to take this into your heart when I say to you that in the beginning, middle, and in the end it's what you say to yourself from deep within that truly matters. Do you even realize how strong that is? If you don't love yourself, how can you expect others to care about you? If you don't believe in yourself, how can you gain the trust and respect of others? How can you get through every day of the rest of your life? Again, you are a person of worth. A person of substance. You have unique abilities and qualities that no one else can match. And, like everybody else, you survived all that you have up to this point because of a little voice, that one thought inside your head. So, think different. Think different, act different, live different. Live better. If what you're doing isn't working, then *do* something different.

America was founded by an impossible dream of a better life for one and all. We didn't even have capable rockets, yet we stretched ourselves with the belief that as a nation we could and would land a man on the moon. *America's Most Wanted* exists thanks to the incredible strength and courage of John Walsh, whose son was murdered. When Martin Luther King stood in front of a mass of people and cried, "I have a dream . . ." he changed the course of history. Because one parent had the guts to make a stand after her child died after being struck down by a drunk driver with known repeated offenses, we now have MADD—Mothers Against Drunk Drivers.

Everything around you—from the water in your home, the paper that you write on, the music from your CD player, to the medicine you take—owes its existence to *someone* taking a no and turning it into a yes. It didn't happen right away, but the smallest amount of optimism can make the world of difference. And if not a difference in the world as a whole, then in you as a person.

So, how do you survive all this negativity? I don't mean to sound crude—as I know of no other way to tiptoe around this matter—but when you hear crap, when you become exposed to filth, or when others go out of their way to fling mud in your direction, you've got to wipe it off and flush everything away, as soon as you can, before it contaminates your brain. Don't allow any crap to get under your skin and into your head! Disinfect yourself, scrape it off, and move on. Replace negativity with something positive. Immediately! Instead of telling yourself no, say maybe, then build up to yes. It's not impossible—hard, yes, but it *is* possible. When disaster befalls you, is there anything you take from it to make yourself better, wiser, more appreciative?

Tell yourself, "I've been through worse before, so I can certainly do this." "I never did mind the *little* things." Take a step back, collect yourself, and calmly state, "It's okay." "It's not that bad." "I'm going to be fine." When you've been thrown on the mat, battered and bruised, vow to yourself, "Righteousness will prevail!" "I know in my heart what is true!" Get into the habit. Deflect the negative. As you would a pestering bug, swat it away.

So, out with crap. If it doesn't do you any good, dump it. Take some action, push that lever, flush it away, and don't look back. Take small steps, every single day of your life, and start taking control of what you say when you talk to yourself.

HELP YOURSELF REMINDERS

* YOUR DAY STARTS WITH *WHAT* YOU SAY TO YOURSELF.
* IMMERSE YOURSELF IN POSITIVE INPUTS.
* FOCUS, FOCUS FOCUS: WHERE ARE YOU AT IN YOUR LIFE? WHAT ARE YOU DOING TO MAKE THINGS BETTER? AND WHERE ARE YOU GOING?
* A LITTLE BIT OF ADVERSITY CAN HELP TO RE-ALIGN YOU, MAKE YOU HUMBLE, AND MAKE YOU WANT IT MORE.
* IT'S MIND OVER MATTER—YOU DON'T MIND ALL THE CRAP "OUT THERE" BECAUSE NONE OF IT MATTERS!

8

Creating Your Own Positive Environment

Now that we know the importance of what we say to ourselves, I want to emphasize another way of deflecting negativity by surrounding yourself with a positive environment that *you create*. As we all know how detrimental a negative setting can be, most of us forget the extreme importance of an affirmative one. When facing the everyday sludge that life can throw at us, I think of a positive environment as a protective shield. Family, friends, loved ones, that close-knit group at work and at church, and other specialized organizations are the perfect outlet to draw inspiration, become motivated, and even gain a shoulder to lean on.

I cannot stress enough the importance of having *someone* not only to talk to or to listen to your fears and dreams, but *someone* who has the same qualities and holds the same set of values as you. As cute as *opposites attract* sounds, I recommend you use more discernment and look at the character of the individual.

As you know, you can't go through life all alone. All of us need assistance and inspiration from time to time. While out in the middle of the ocean, Brad Van Liew drew strength from his wife and a small band of friends constantly pulling for him and, as Mr. Van Liew put it, in some cases giving him a kick in the pants.

We've all heard those seemingly insignificant words *I'm proud of you, Don't give up, You can do it,* but isn't it amazing the absolute power of those words coming from someone you know and trust? To me *that's* the heart of a positive environment. Being with those you feel safe and secure with, enough to open up to, to expose your inner self, for the purpose of empowering you to become a better person. *That's* the value of a positive environment!

If anyone knows about the benefits of receiving help from a realistic, nurturing environment among close family and friends, it's Toni Braxton. Even though Ms. Braxton had two top-selling, multiplatinum albums and was the recipient of five Grammys, there was a time when she wasn't sure she would ever record another album. When Ms. Braxton found herself in the middle of a bitter contract dispute with her record label, which in turn led her to file for bankruptcy, she was humiliated to the point that even her Grammy awards were stickered with price tags. Yet it was her friends and family who helped Toni with that little encouragement when she needed it. Record producer and ally Kenny "Babyface" Edmonds said to her, "You know how to produce yourself. Go do it." For Toni to have someone like Babyface, whom she looked up to as a big brother in the business, "that made me feel real good." With a little inspiration Ms. Braxton is now a stronger, wiser person and after four years has another top-selling album.

But a positive environment isn't all candy canes, soda pops, and warm cuddles. As much as we use it to draw encouragement from, it can also be a hard dose of reality for us when needed. After years of living an internal hell, Oprah Winfrey's life turned for the better when she moved in with her father, a caring but "no-nonsense" individual. Through the many interviews I've seen and read about Ms. Winfrey, she credits her father's tough love for helping make her the woman she is today. While surrounding her with encouragement and praise, it is said that Ms. Winfrey's father also made sure that Oprah read anything she could lay her hands on, and above all expected nothing but the best from her.

What's great about a positive environment is surrounding yourself with those whom you trust, but is not about being told only what you want to hear. It's the reality of the truth. As my lovely bride likes to point out, this is one of the many benefits of the institution called marriage. As much as I do as an author, presenter, and comedic storyteller, my wife is always happy to inform me when I have floundered; when I've stepped or am about to step past the edge. Why? Because she knows my capabilities and expects nothing less. And because we trust each other, I not only can open up to her all the more, but can value the sometimes-hard-to-swallow critiques that in the end keep me grounded, more focused, and a better person as a whole.

Real Life Resources

But in today's world there are a great number of folks who aren't content with the invaluable everyday resources that are so readily available to them. Rather than take advice from people who actually, truly know them, these folks prefer to wait for the next motivational, all-knowing, quasi-immortal guru to sweep them off their feet and have them live in some distant paradise where they can dedicate themselves to their "conduit of peace." Now, with all due respect, if that's what adults unequivocally wish to do with their lives and they truly believe in that certain cause, and if it makes them happy, well, then, more power to them. I am only trying to emphasize how many times over the years I have seen seemingly lost people throw their lives and worldly possessions away in the vain hope of finding their way through to some divinelike environment. Why travel across the desert if your well is right in front of you?

As mentioned in the very beginning of this book, no one has all the answers. And I highly advise you to stay clear of those who righteously claim they do. The truth is, those seemingly mundane words like, "Come on, don't quit," "Everything's gonna be great," "I believe in you," are the ones that have an extraordinary impact on our lives!

Off the top of your head, how many teachers can you name? Now, how many of those close friends can you recall for every class you had in school, or those select few you were just dying to have a date with? I may be wrong here, but you probably came up with more teachers than those friends whom at the time you couldn't live without. Why? Because *they* were the ones who truly had a genuine influence on your life. As much as we habitually draw from bad experiences, I think it's time we turned that around and tapped—if not *drilled*—into those positive former experiences as well. You'll find those experiences from everyday folks who know you, who don't have all the answers or even the responses you wish to hear, but are definitely the folks making a world of difference in your life today!

So don't wait for the next guru messiah to provide you with divine guidance for every one of life's encounters. That's not going to happen. For me, what I've found that does in fact work every single time is drawing strength and encouragement from myself and a close group of folks that I have a relationship with. Those folks whom I trust and whose opinions I value.

In all my years of helping others I've met so many who said, "I gotta meet Oprah, so *she* can help me!" Or "When I see Arnold, *he'll* become my workout coach!" I realize this may sound obvious, and not to burst anyone's bubble, but it ain't gonna happen! Even with the slightest of chances of bumping into Ms. Winfrey, Mr. Schwarzenegger, Colin Powell, or even someone else who may have had similar experiences to yours, they can only give you a fraction of their time. And even if they throw you a piece of advice such as "Keep a good spirit," "Maintain a healthy body for a healthy mind," "Pursue a solid education," or "I'm sorry you went through that situation, too," there is no way you can have an ongoing affiliation with folks such as these. Again, too many individuals put *their faith in others* rather than in themselves or what's in front of them and readily available. I freely admit that every one of those folks deserves respect, has an incredible message to share with the world, and can *help* inspire us to better ourselves, but that's as far as it goes. Do you have Oprah's cell phone number and can you call her anytime you wish? Can you page Colin Powell whenever you feel the need? No, you can't. *But* you can turn to a family member, someone at work, or that one close friend of yours, for advice. A twelve-step sponsor is only a phone call away. A hug of encouragement is just an arm's reach away. But believing in yourself is the first step.

After all I've just said, if folks still only place little value on the ordinary positive surroundings, then I ask how was I—after the extreme negative environment I've been subjected to—able to become a kind and loving husband and father, and a decent member of our society? With years of enduring psychological and physical torture from my deranged mother, and even while in foster care when certain individuals went out of their way to brag openly about my limited chances of any "normal social adjustment" (while being kind enough to bestow their own credit on my inner determination), it was in fact my foster parents who took me into their homes—when no one else would have me—and who not only made me a part of their family, but gave me a strong sense of values that I could draw from. As a teenager, when I stepped out of line, my hard-nosed social workers would scold me by asking, "Aren't you better than that?" While in the air force, when I had to take a prealgebra class for the third time, there was this one instructor with the patience of a saint who said the one thing that enabled me to understand the workings of numbers, even though he had stated the same thing to me a hundred plus times before. It has been and always will be true that the resources of a positive environment are what are in and around you. If you can pick and choose who and what to stay away from when it comes to staying clear of a negative setting, you can certainly take advantage of selecting from a positive one.

I believe that for every single negative you hear about yourself, it takes dozens of positives to counter that one appalling spoken word or that singular bad experience. In my case, I was able to absorb, to draw from every single seemingly ordinary constructive event, which in turn propelled me to become the person I am today. That is the honest-to-God truth! It wasn't meeting some Hollywood celebrity, pretentious radio talk-show host, or that onetime weekend walking on coals that left such an extraordinary effect on my life. All of those may have somehow affected our lives, but fleetingly at best. And you deserve better than that.

I fully realize that not all things work for or apply to all people. I'm sure, though in my heart I hope it's not true, that there are some who feel they have no one to turn to for support that *all* of us need. For that I am truly sorry. There have been many, many times in my life, just as in everyone's, when I have felt dejected and completely isolated. As crazy as this sounds, with all the 900 adult entertainment and psychic telephone services there are, I wish there were a 1-900-*Have-a-Nice-Day* line. Wouldn't it be great to pick up the line, get something off your chest, and feel just a little bit better afterward, knowing you're not alone, the world's not going to end, and tomorrow is indeed another day? (This is one of the reasons I would love to have my own radio show!) Heck, in our hypersonic telecommunication age it might be a good thing! And yet, if one looks hard enough, there are in fact many outreach services readily available within one's community. Help is there for those who seek it.

And, after all of this, if some folks still feel they do not have any positive elements in their lives, still feel alone and worthless, then with all due respect I say: "Get off your butt and help out others who are worse off than you!" For folks who think they don't have enough, I recommend spending a few hours a week helping out at a homeless shelter. For those who believe they're all alone, I advise manning the phones at suicide prevention or runaway hotlines. Once I had a person so wrapped up in his own despair that I took him to visit children diagnosed with cancer, AIDS, and other terminal diseases. Thankfully, afterward this gentleman sobbed, "What do *I* have to complain about?"

Indeed.

You and I are not alone. We are not the only ones with insurmountable troubles, for there is always someone somewhere who's worse off than ourselves. Not to sound hard nosed, but I highly recommend the film *Saving Private Ryan*. After watching the first thirty minutes, I realized—even after all I have been put through—that I have nothing, and I mean nothing, to complain about. I don't mean to confuse anyone, for it's great and necessary to get things off our chests. And I highly recommend doing just that; however, I only wish to make the point that as individuals we have to make the most of what we have, and when you reach out to assist others, when *you* become that mentor to others, you are in fact creating your own positive environment!

Look at Oprah! She had serious issues, received everyday, commonsense guidance, and is now helping millions! Colin Powell, raised in the ghetto, worked incredibly hard to receive his education, and is now in charge of "America's Promise, The Alliance for Youth" giving his all for other children to better themselves. Nelson Mandela was imprisoned for many years because of his race and his political views, yet became the president of the country that had persecuted him! It all began with the courage to make that change.

Creating your positive environment begins with the little things, so, as I have already advised, take consistent small daily steps. I again recommend the same for your own setting. Once a day, do at least three nice things for others. Just three little seemingly insignificant things every day for the rest of your life. Open the door for that person. When someone cuts you off in traffic, spare your energy by not giving him the bird. If you see someone who can use some spare change, buy her a Happy Meal.

Feeling bad about your own esteem? Then compliment others: "And good morning to you, Denise. Love your hair!" "Hi, Bob, now that's a sharp tie!" "Hey, girlfriend, where did you get those shoes?" "Hello, Matt. Nice toupee!"

That positive environment always has and always will begin with you! And it's what you say to yourself that leads you either to victory or defeat; happiness or despair; mind over matter.

Self-Evaluation

When you watch what you say when you talk to yourself, *listen* to what is being said. Again I know it sounds a little foolish, but do just that. Since listening is the most neglected of all communications skills and we now know the extreme importance of our initial internal thoughts, take it to the next step and improve your own position.

Start with this: Next Monday morning when you go to work, off to school, or do whatever you do, *listen* to what *others say* when they talk about *themselves*. Do they complain much about every single insignificant thing in their lives? Are they constantly making excuses? Are they happy? Do they seem fulfilled or content in any way? What about their body language? Watch their breathing. Is it strained or labored? Are their shoulders hunched over? Do they have bags under their eyes from lack of a sound sleep? Observe how these folks react with others and how productive they actually are. Given, on Mondays, for a fair amount of us, it's hard to get back into the swing of things. And everybody has bad days and even a run of hard times, but over time folks like these are so despondent with themselves, they can barely accomplish anything outside of their problematic realm.

On the other hand, have you seen those people who are constantly chipper? Nothing gets them that down. When push comes to shove these individuals hunker down and do whatever it takes to accomplish their tasks. At times these folks seem so overly optimistic that you're not quite sure if they're on some unlicensed medication. They have dreams and wide-eyed ambitions, and even when bad luck or negative situations befall them, these people seemingly brush it off as if it weren't a big deal. They have the eyes that always seem to be smiling. For them the glass is half full. They create their own environment from within. Their enthusiasm is infectious. And those are the folks whom you want to watch. They are the ones going places!

Now for some, these folks might seem downright odd. But ask yourself: out of the two examples, whom would your rather surround yourself with?

As you know, the brain thinks in pictures rather than words and as you visualize something good or bad, the brain in a sense leads you in that direction. This is why it is imperative for you to control how and what you think! And to stay positive is to do exactly that. Taking control of the everyday turmoil, not allowing things to get you down, destroy you, or take away your passion for a fulfilled life!

When I think of one person who is the master of hard work, envisioning his own destiny years ahead himself, I think of Arnold Schwarzenegger. If you want to see someone with a confident attitude, watch this man whenever he's on the television talk-show circuit.

Years ago, when I didn't even know Arnold's name, I happened to catch him on an afternoon talk show that went something like this: "So, Arnold, tell us about your latest film." "You know I'm so excited to be here. I tell you, for years I worked hard on my body, chiseling every inch to perfection, knowing all the time that I would use it as a tool to get me into movies in America. For me that was my big dream. That's why I'm a success. I see nothing in front of me but endless opportunity. In this film I push myself, I work hard to ensure I have the best body, for my fans expect nothing less. You will also see so much action, you'll feel as if you're in the movie yourself. I've never seen or been a part of anything like it. It's just incredible. And now that I've established myself as an actor, I plan to explore new boundaries, different character dimensions, the works. In fact, in my next film . . ."

Wow! As shamelessly "pluggish" as Mr. Schwarzenegger may be, listen carefully. He tells you where he was, what he has just accomplished, and what he plans on accomplishing next. "When I see it in my mind, it becomes crystallized, and I take whatever steps necessary to make it happen. I follow through!" The intensity of his eyes and his body language match his enthusiasm, not necessarily for the film he's promoting, but more so on his attitude about his life in general. When he talks about his past, one of his hands is about knee level. Then when Arnold discusses what he has just accomplished, his hand rises to his chest. But by the time he tells the audience his goals for the future, his hand is just above his eyes and all the time his smile widens with each and every incline. Besides his lovely wife and children, Arnold claims his biggest asset is his limitless positive internal environment.

So what's your internal environment like? When you observe others, what can you learn about yourself in the process? Do you needlessly rant and complain? Do you make infinite excuses? Do you find yourself too defensive? Or are you optimistic? When the going gets tough do you tell yourself that you will do whatever it takes to make things happen?

When you're feeling blue, do you allow that to pull you down, or do you make the most of it? Do you go out of your way to brighten other people's day, rather than wallow in your own abyss of doom and gloom? Again, it's up to you. It's all a matter of weeding out the bad and cultivating more productive thoughts. And just like pulling weeds, you have to get to the root of the problem; otherwise that weed, that self-doubt, that negative programming, will spring back up and choke off the flower that can blossom for you in the future. Be consistent. Apply that "weed off" whenever you feel the need. Every day see the brighter side of things. Continually tell yourself how lucky you are, how good your life is right now, and how things can only get better.

Don't wait! Now, starting NOW—not tomorrow, next week, next month, or even next year—THINK DIFFERENTLY! Deflect all that exterior crap that you probably have little control over in the first place and begin by instructing yourself that things aren't that bad. When others put you down, smile inside while telling yourself you are better than that. When others laugh at your delusions of grandeur, tell yourself you will give it all you have, you don't mind paying the price, and how much you will enjoy the journey.

I promise you this: If you carry a bad attitude, you have no chance of being happy, let alone living up to your full potential and achieving your greatness. With a positive mind and a nurturing environment, what can you not truly accomplish? You keep a clear head and an optimistic attitude—day in and day out—and you *will* see a miraculous difference! This I guarantee!

The truth: You may not get the "brass ring," but you will live a better life! Remember, it takes about twenty-seven separate facial muscles to frown and about nineteen to smile. So reach down deep inside. No matter how hard life hits you, no matter how long it takes, do whatever it takes. And smile, smile, smile!

I beg of you to take this with you always: Help Yourself . . . to a life you are not only capable of living, but are worthy of living. *It's all in your mind . . . that's where everything matters.*

HELP YOURSELF REMINDERS

* DRAW SUPPORT FROM THOSE YOU KNOW AND TRUST.
* CONSISTENTLY KEEP YOURSELF IN CHECK WITH THE ENVIRONMENT THAT YOU CREATE.

EPILOGUE

One Final Note

Congratulations. *You* did it. You stuck it out, you took the time, dedication, and the energy to enhance your life and I am proud of you! You made a commitment to read the material and you followed through. In this day and age, with so much happening to us all at such tremendous speed, I fully realize and appreciate how precious your time is. Of the endless number of self-help books out there, you were willing to invest some of your hard-earned money and take a chance on this one, and that means the world to me. I only hope you are willing to extract and implement parts of this book that apply to your life now and to come, so as to make a significant difference in you. That is my sole desire.

In the first section we learned that all of us, every single person on this planet, face difficult situations of one degree or another, and that we cannot move forward unless we free ourselves from the shackles of our past. We know that unless we have the knowledge, courage, and constant discipline to maintain our distance from negative settings, there is a chance—but not the excuse—that we can become a carbon copy of that environment. That above all, bad things happen to decent folks every single day, and feelings of animosity or revenge, at any level, do no one any good and can either take away our wholesomeness or kill us a little bit each and every day . . . until we become what we once detested.

We realized that if we have no goals or even the slightest amount of ambition, we will end up going nowhere. That what truly matters for nearly all of us is actually the everyday simple things that are so readily available. That for everything in life we desire, we have to be willing to forfeit something for our cause. And we know that achieving enormous goals requires unyielding dedication and patience, coupled with a fair amount of luck.

That in the end, the sincere appreciation of who we are and what we have thus far should suffice, and that anything extra that comes into our lives is a bonus, which can only make our lives the more enjoyable. That diligent labor is important, yet making the most of our days by doing things that make us feel fulfilled is just as vital. That a sustained, proactive environment not only nurtures, but can be used as a shield so we can live with less turmoil and fewer distractions. How a slight amount of negativity is not only inescapable, but in fact can be used as a catalyst to better ourselves. That a steadfast, strong, positive attitude inside ourselves or when we deal with the world around us makes all the difference.

We see that America is truly the land where God has

shed His grace on thee. Yet perhaps the extraordinary thing about America is not solely its boundless opportunities for one and all, but the guaranteed, undisputable right of the pursuit of happiness. It by no means implies the absolute right for an auspicious life, but rather to simply live a life as we choose. If one wishes to fulfill this promise and be happy, America is a phenomenal place to be.

Every single one of us knows something about resilience. As you were reading, did you tell yourself, "Hey, I've been through worse than that," or "If that person can do it, then I certainly can too!"? Did you find that *you* in fact have some of the same persevering traits as those who were used as examples? Did you rediscover that even in the midst of adversity you are not counted out unless *you* say so? That no matter the past or present situation, you in fact have ownership to your life and deserve to live your life on your own terms?

However, if there was one theme that I want to shine throughout this book, the singular thread that I hope you will weave into your life is the fact that nothing can dominate the hunger, the unstoppable drive, of the human spirit. *Nothing*. Not the test of time, any technology mankind can devise, or any form of oppression—no matter how monumental. Nothing comes close to matching the determination from within you! If you walk away with nothing else, please take that knowledge with you. The only element stopping you is you.

But now that our time together is through, I must emphasize that now it's up to you. Now is the time to follow through, to go the distance, to activate yourself on what you have now acquired. As I have previously stated, this book, myself, or others you know can only propel you so far. If you feel excited, ready to jump up and tackle the world, understand that that stimulation will soon fade. Don't get me wrong; being enthusiastic is great, but don't get so wound up that you use up all your energy ahead of time. Or if you hit a few bumps in life, or run into a roadblock, you turn away, flee, and give up. Personally, I think you've come too far to do that.

My advice: Stay on course. Take a stand and implement a change. Just be consistent in your endeavors. Want it, crave it, do it . . . on a daily basis. Like brushing your teeth whenever you get up each day and before going to bed: take the time required to hit those "hard-to-reach places," then walk away with something to smile about. Dedicate yourself to your changes, so they become a part of your life.

Again the changes may seem small and even insignificant. When we brush our teeth, we don't always walk away with a blinding radiant smile, but imagine not only how our smile would look but the overall condition of our mouths and gums if we did not consistently brush? Trust me, overall you will be so much better off by stepping out of that comfort zone and applying yourself in a positive direction. I'm not going to sugarcoat this: You will teeter and even fall, but simply stand up, brush yourself off, and be all the wiser next time.

I fully realize *Help Yourself* has dealt with some fairly serious topics. My intention was to show you that life, even with all its fury, *does not* have to be so arduous. That even in the midst of chaos, the world is not going to end. With positive perseverance, things do get better. And how can you be an astute businessperson, a loving, guiding parent, an intimate partner, a good student, or live your life as an everyday productive person if you do not take care of your most important asset: yourself?! The answer is you can't. So as much as you apply yourself, don't forget to stop and pick more daisies along the way. Enjoy! Go out and have an ice cream, and hold the hand of someone you love. Do it today!

I only ask one more thing from you: Please don't let it end here. Digest what you can and skim through the parts when you need more clarification or that extra shot in the arm. Just don't quit on yourself. Remember that all of us are worthy and we all deserve to be happy. All you have to do now is do what has to be done. As the beloved Ms. Winfrey once stated, "Now that you know better, do better."

As I close, please permit me to say that it has been an honor for me. I pray the time we spent together will enable you to live your life with a little more dignity, honor, and sense of conviction. If you ever think you are unworthy, that you're reaching too far, that you will never be happy, do me this favor as you read these words:

Imagine a small boy who lives in the bottom of a cold, dark basement. A lonely, terrified child with yellowish skin, wounds and bruises all over his body. A child with no one and nothing to turn to, who is either doomed to die or destined to spend the rest of his life in a living hell. This was the life for a child called "It."

After everything, against all odds, if that little boy can now live a happy, fulfilled, productive life, with all due respect, what is stopping you? In the end there is little that is insurmountable if you are simply willing to help yourself.

With all of my heart I wish you Godspeed on all your journeys and God's blessings on your endeavors. I wish you my very best. Live a good life. Be happy.

Dave Pelzer

About the Author

A retired air force aircrew member, Dave played a major role in Operations Just Cause, Desert Shield, and Desert Storm. Dave was selected for the unique task of mid-air refueling of the once highly secretive SR-71 Blackbird and the F-117 Stealth Fighter. While serving in the air force, Dave worked in juvenile hall and other programs involving "youth at risk" throughout California.

Dave's exceptional accomplishments include commendations from Presidents Reagan, Bush, and Clinton, as well as other heads of state. While maintaining an international active-duty flight schedule, Dave was the recipient of the 1990 J. C. Penney Golden Rule Award, making him the California Volunteer of the Year. In 1993, Dave was honored as one of the Ten Outstanding Young Americans (TOYA), joining a distinguished group of alumni that includes Chuck Yeager, Christopher Reeve, Anne Bancroft, John F. Kennedy, Orson Welles, and Walt

Disney. In 1994, Dave was the *only* American to be selected as one of The Outstanding Young Persons of the World (TOYP), for his efforts involving child-abuse awareness and prevention, as well as for instilling resilience in others. During the centennial Olympic Games, Dave was a torch bearer, carrying the coveted flame.

Dave is one of the only authors to have three books simultaneously on the *New York Times* best-seller list. Dave's first book, *A Child Called "It,"* has been on the *New York Times* best-seller list for over two years. Dave's second book, *The Lost Boy,* has been on the same list for over one year and Dave's third book, *A Man Named Dave,* was an instant *New York Times* best-seller.

Dave is currently working on his next book, *The Privilege of Youth*. His future works will then include themes of humor in relationships.

When not on the road or with his wife, Marsha, or son, Stephen, Dave is either traipsing through Carmel or living a quiet life in Southern California, with his box turtle named Chuck.

You can visit Dave's Web site at **www.davepelzer.com** for more on Dave.

Some of the names in this book have been changed in order to protect the dignity and privacy of others.

KEYNOTES

Dave's unique and inspirational outlook on life, coupled with his "Robin Williams" like wit and sense of humor, entertain and encourage business professionals to overcome any obstacle while living life to its fullest. Dave is a living testament of resilience, faith in humanity, and personal responsibility. This is what makes him one of the most exceptional and unequaled personalities in corporate America today.

Dave also provides specific programs to those who work in the human services and educational fields.

For additional information on having Dave for your group, please call us, fax us, or visit our Web site at:

D-ESPRIT
P.O. Box 1846
Rancho Mirage, CA 92270
Phone: 760-321-4452
Fax: 760-321-6842
www.davepelzer.com

And for those who wish to write letters to Dave, please include a SASE and keep in mind that due to the large volume of letters we receive daily, we will not be able to answer every letter. But we sincerely thank you for your time and support.